RELIGIOUS VOCATIONS

A Text - book for the Church "Class in
Occupations" and Hand - book of
Information for Pastors, Parents,
Teachers, and other Counsellors of
Christian Youth.

by

Frank M. Lowe, Jr., A.M., Ph.D.

First Fruits Press
Wilmore, Kentucky
c2015

Religious vocations by Frank M. Lowe, Jr.

First Fruits Press, ©2016
Previously published by the International Society of Christian Endeavor, ©1928.

ISBN: 9781621713616 (print), 9781621713623 (digital)

Digital version at http://place.asburyseminary.edu/christianendeavorbooks/41/

For all other uses, contact:

First Fruits Press
B.L. Fisher Library
Asbury Theological Seminary
204 N. Lexington Ave.
Wilmore, KY 40390
http://place.asburyseminary.edu/firstfruits

Lowe, Frank Melville, 1888-1977.
  Religious vocations: a text-book for the church "class in occupations" and hand-book of information of pastors, parents, teachers, and other counsellors of Christian youth / by Frank M. Lowe, Jr. -- Wilmore, Kentucky : First Fruits Press, ©2016.
        230 pages ; 21 cm.
        Reprint. Previously published: Boston : International Society of Christian Endeavor, ©1928.
        ISBN - 13: 9781621713616 (pbk.)
        1. Clergy--Office. 2. Vocation, Ecclesiastical. 3. Missionaries. 4. Church work. I. Title.
BV660.L65 2016   262.1

Cover design by Jonathan Ramsay

asburyseminary.edu
800.2ASBURY
204 North Lexington Avenue
Wilmore, Kentucky 40390

First Fruits
THE ACADEMIC OPEN PRESS OF ASBURY SEMINARY

First Fruits Press
The Academic Open Press of Asbury Theological Seminary
204 N. Lexington Ave., Wilmore, KY 40390
859-858-2236
first.fruits@asburyseminary.edu
asbury.to/firstfruits

.

RELIGIOUS VOCATIONS

A Text-book for the Church "Class in Occupations" and Hand-book of Information for Pastors, Parents, Teachers, and other Counsellors of Christian Youth.

BY

FRANK M. LOWE, JR., A.M., Ph.D.

1928

INTERNATIONAL SOCIETY OF CHRISTIAN ENDEAVOR

BOSTON   CHICAGO

PRINTED IN THE U. S. A.

To

DEAN GRANVILLE D. EDWARDS

Teacher, Counsellor, Friend

INTRODUCTION

PURPOSE

To give needed information to Christian young people facing life decisions, and to provide parents, teachers, pastors, and others with a handbook of reference is the purpose of this book.

SCOPE

To set forth the programme of work, the number of workers, the salary, the openings, the joys, the drawbacks, the essential preparation, and the desirable personality in the worker in each of a number of main types of salaried service among ministers, missionaries, and laymen in positions within or closely affiliated with the evangelical Protestant church is its scope.

METHOD

"Job analysis," based upon a study of original sources, interviews, and returns from representative groups of workers in each occupation, has been used as far as possible throughout the study.

ACKNOWLEDGMENTS

Several hundred individuals have given courteous co-operation and genuine help, sincerely appreciated. Especial thanks are due Dr. David Snedden, of Teachers' College; to Dr. John M. Brewer, of Harvard, whose stimulating teaching of vocational guidance inspired the idea; to Mr. E. W. Weaver, for help both in and out of the class room; and to Dr. Daniel A. Poling. I am indebted most of all for constant assistance and encouragement to my mother.

CONCLUSION

This is, apparently, one of the first attempts to gather together in one book, from the point of view of the vocational guidance movement, without the motive of propaganda, the occupational opportunities in religious work. The endeavor has been to make an accurate and unbiased approach, while retaining the full flavor of romance, which never can be analyzed out of the great adventure of full-time Christian service.

FRANK M. LOWE, JR.

New York City.

CONTENTS

INTRODUCTORY

*"Trusting in the Lord Jesus Christ
for strength, I promise Him that I will
strive from this day forth so to shape
the plans of my life that I may give
myself to full-time Christian service."*

RELIGIOUS VOCATIONS

CHAPTER I

"VOCATIONAL GUIDANCE" FOR RELIGIOUS VOCATIONS

I. The Vocational Guidance Movement

Of the million early-teen-age boys and girls who annually set out on industrial careers in the United States, it is safe to say that more than half find employment by taking to the street and hunting jobs; that more than four out of five accept blind-alley positions, affording little advancement, where three to seven out of ten are quickly dissatisfied; and that, in most cases, the choice of work being left to chance and accident, "the job chooses the vocation."[1]

If these new juvenile job-hunters for one year should set out upon their vocational journey from the Pennsylvania Station, New York City, they would form a continuous stream of outgoing traffic which it would take the normal facilities of this world-terminal three weeks, moving day and night, to handle.[2] Most of these youthful travellers would arrive at the station unprepared for the trip, without any idea of their destination, and would step up to the window, blindfolded, to grab a ticket for any point which Agent Luck might

[1]Brewer, John M., "Vocational Guidance Movement," Macmillan, N. Y., 1919.

[2]Based upon daily average, 1920, estimated by David N. Bell, P. T. M.

11

happen to hand out. Under such circumstances, who could doubt that many would eventually reach unsuitable destinations, to be dissatisfied, ineffective workers, or to become vocational hoboes?

History. This indicates slightly, and in one feature only, something of the problem which faces the American schools and which has created, as one factor in its solution, the vocational guidance movement. Under the early leadership of Frank Parsons, and later of Meyer Bloomfield, the Boston Vocation Bureau, established in 1908, proved the successful missionary for a cause, already appearing in some quarters, and for which the whole nation was more or less ready. To-day a dozen progressive cities maintain vocation bureaus, a score of colleges and universities offer suitable courses, and hundreds of high schools carry out vocational guidance programmes.

Purpose. Briefly stated, vocational guidance aims to serve the individual and society by helping young people help themselves to choose wisely, to prepare adequately for, to launch successfully into, and to advance consistently through progressive readjustments, into satisfying vocational life. This it proposes to bring about by cultivating in the child as early as possible a vocational attitude. Just as other teachers promote the growth of a habit of scientific method, or a taste for poetry, or an ear for music, the guidance expert endeavors to train in the pupil an appreciative eye for work and workers. A growing boy is on his way to work, and it will save time and waste later if he can make up his mind as he goes what he wants to do when he gets there.

Method. In detail, the vocational guidance programme includes six or seven steps, ranging from pre-
vocational, "tryout" courses in the grades and the
junior high school to employment supervision after the
worker is placed. In a general way the earlier measures, those functioning in the school, may be divided
into the formational and the diagnostic. In the case
of the latter type, which have to do with examining
a person and pronouncing vocational sentence upon
him, the counsellor is on very thin ice. Although psychological tests are the rage, the fact remains that in
selecting positions for persons, psychology has attained
scant scientific progress.[1] Since diagnosis by charac-
ter-analysis is almost as much discredited, it is the
informational feature which vocational guidance emphasizes, a major method being the "class in occupations," now increasingly offered by schools throughout the country.

While it is only one of several activities the class
in occupations may be taken to represent the spirit of
the movement as a whole. The members of such a
class, in addition to interviewing workers, listening to
addresses by workers, observing in industrial plants,
reading about vocations, and studying the right steps
in the vocational progress of the individual, take up
systematically a survey of vocations, asking about
each such questions as these suggested by Dr. Brewer[2]:

1. What service to society is rendered by those
in the occupation?

2. What things are actually done by a person

---

[1] Ayres, L. P., "Psychological Tests in Vocational Guidance,"
Journ. Educ. Psy., April, 1913.

[2] Brewer, John M., "Material for the Class in Occupations," Bureau of Vocational Guidance, Harvard University, 1920.

in this calling? (a) Make a list of them. (b) Outline a typical day's work.

3. What are the main advantages of the occupation? (a) Service to humanity? (b) Chance to learn? (c) Demand for workers? (d) Steady work? (e) Growing importance? (f) Interesting work? (g) Promotions? (h) Friends, associates? (i) Hours? (j) Vacations? (k) Good living? (l) Healthy work? (m) Ethical conditions? (n) Other points?

4. What are its disadvantages and problems?

5. What preparation is necessary or desirable?

6. What are other requirements for success?

7. What income is to be expected, at first, later?

8. What effect of occupation on social, civic, physical, recreational, and moral life of worker?

The purpose of this class, however, is not so much to give specific vocational information as to develop a vocational consciousness and a habit for job analysis. Especial emphasis is placed upon the desirability of a broad educational background as well as of thorough vocational preparation, the conviction being that a teen-age child is never so well "placed" as when placed in school. With such an alert attitude awakened and trained early in life, a normal boy is more certain to find himself, and thus in time to prepare better to make his life count most. This is the goal of the vocational guidance movement, for it is based squarely upon the proposition that the whole world works and that to make better workmen is to make a better world.

II. NEED FOR GUIDANCE IN RELIGIOUS VOCATIONS.

It is the application in the religious field of the spirit
and method of vocational guidance which this book
undertakes. By putting Dr. Brewer's questions to the
religious callings, it is hoped to add to the enlarging
number of life-career text-books one suitable for a
"class in religious occupations." This undertaking is
new. Although many books, setting forth the programme needs, and unfinished task of Christianity in
every field of religious service are increasingly available, these describe only indirectly the types and characteristics of the work from the worker's point of
view. In every case the motive has been missionary
propaganda rather than a contribution to the literature of vocational guidance. Religious activities in
the present case are to be considered not from the
point of view of function but of vocation, not of work
but of worker, not of need but of opportunity. In
making such an approach, one of several questions
which suggest themselves is, "What are religious
vocations?"

Religious Vocations Defined. "Go start a savings
bank," was the answer of Professor T. N. Carver of
Harvard to a religious worker who asked in what calling he could best serve society. This reply illustrates
the modern conception of the sacredness of all produc-
tive labor, of the tendency to consider that the best
way to serve God is by serving mankind, that the best
way to serve mankind is by producing goods, that
therefore every producer is potentially a Christian
workman, and, accordingly, that every position filled
by a Christian is a Christian vocation. Undoubtedly,

all legitimate callings may be filled to the glory of God. Nevertheless, certain types of work are religious per se; that is, they are not only subjectively Christian because of the Christian motive behind them, but they are objectively Christian, furthering directly through organized church and interchurch activities the democracy of God. It is with these clear-cut, full-time, salaried religious vocations that this study deals.[1]

With regard to such callings, do Christian young people need information and guidance? How many of the nearly three-quarter million[2] secondary Sunday-school pupils in the United States precede their entrance into vocational life with any systematic consideration of the occupational opportunities in religious work? Even of those who choose a religious career, how many do so after a careful study of its programme and routine, its difficulties as well as its satisfactions, and its requirement as to personality and preparation? To these questions no statistical answers are forthcoming, but it may be affirmed in general that the lack, especially of high-grade workers, the unpopularity of religious careers among young people, and the excessive "mortality" among those who make decisions, indicate an emphatic need to replace, or at least to supplement, the present all-too-prevalent, spasmodic, emotional appeal with a systematic, sober survey of the field of religious vocations.

Life-Work Recruit Movement. Nothing emphasizes more the urgency for wise guidance within the church

---

[1] For definition of "vocation" see Snedden, D., "Vocational Education," Macmillan, N. Y., 1920, p. 398.

[2] Report of Fourteenth International Sunday-School Convention, Chicago, 1914, gave 641,441 pupils in the secondary Division, in organized classes alone.

than the present interest in recruiting religious workers, which, at least up to the point of securing decisions, is strongly stressed by the young people's societies. In 1913 the United Society of Christian Endeavor, adopting a plan already tried by the Ohio Christian Endeavor Union, organized the Christian Endeavor Life-Work Recruit Movement, planning to enroll all Endeavorers who would pledge themselves to try to shape their life-plans to enter full-time salaried Christian service. Since that time Christian Endeavor conventions, county, district, State, and international, have utilized the "decision service" to such good advantage that thousands have enrolled. In 1927 a Department of Christian Vocations was added, to assist young people in choosing the proper vocations, but placing special emphasis on those definitely related to Christian work.

A similar movement is the Life-Service League of the Baptist Young People's Union, its object being to present definitely and forcefully to Baptist young people "the call of God for Kingdom service in this hour of the world's need." In providing for the recruit's signature, regarded not as a pledge but rather as a declaration of purpose only, this organization submits three different cards, which list in all thirty-eight types of service.

The Life-Work Department of the Epworth League mobilizes its force largely through summer institutes. At these, of which many are held annually throughout the United States, the full one-day programme provides a forty-minute life-workers' class, in which a beginning is made in giving vocational information. Also at local evening institutes more or less emphasis is placed upon a summons-to-service address and the signing of decision cards. These cards are of two kinds, the indefinite "I will find myself," and the definite, "I have found myself" decision. Of the two types, the central office now has record of more than 8,000.[1] No one can doubt that this wide activity in enlistment on the part of the young people's movement would be more far-reaching and more permanent if it could build upon the firm foundation of a comprehensive, popular class in religious vocations.

Student Volunteer Movement. To have helped place upward of nine thousand volunteers in the foreign field is the achievement of this organization, which, beginning in 1886 at Mt. Hermon, Mass., with a handful of students whom Dwight L. Moody called in conference, has grown until to-day its paid staff includes, in addition to fifteen or twenty headquarters and travelling secretaries, a clerical force alone of twenty. At its convention in Des Moines in 1920, 5,428 of the 6,890 delegates were college students. In addition to the direct influence of the conventions, the movement has 564 volunteer bands in the colleges and universities of the country; while its publications alone number no less than twenty-eight books, seventy-five pamphlets, and a quarterly magazine. This enterprise, this central labor bureau for the missionary harvest field, which so splendidly faces the college youth of America, and increasingly of the world, with the challenge of Christian service, has a singular opportunity and necessity to promote, even more than it has religious vocational guidance.

Y. M. C. A. Programme. The Boys' Work Division of the International committee has adopted a com-

---

[1] Information kindly furnished by W. E. J. Gratz, Secretary of the Department of Institutes and Life Work, Chicago.

prehensive, five-year policy, 1920-1925, for enlisting boys in Christian callings. Considering its legitimate field, the more than 600,000 high-school boys in the United States, it plans to reach large numbers of these young men through find-yourself campaigns, State and county older boys' conferences, and older boys' life-work conferences, as well as through the Hi-Y activities. Personal interviews and follow-up are to receive special emphasis, and the whole campaign fits into the programme of vocational guidance which the association has already undertaken. Through its far-reaching, effective organization, the Y. M. C. A. has unusual opportunity for carrying out a programme which does not contemplate over-emphasizing but simply duly-emphasizing the call for service in order "to discover those whose talents and qualifications fit them particularly for lives of Christian leadership." The revised list now contains three hundred names.

The Sunday-School Attitude. Although some denominational departments of religious education, notably that of the Disciples of Christ, report great interest in recruiting, for the most part, an emphasis upon life-decisions has not gained great headway in the church school. Probably as a protest against methods which sometimes have appeared like unwarranted exploitation of adolescent nature, the tendency has been rather the other way. The last report of the young people's division to the executive committee of the International Sunday-School Association contains in its entire review of activities for the year only one reference to the presentation of Christian life-work, and that only as a possible feature of a future programme for the college Sunday-school conference, reaching a small and highly selected group. However, leaders in religious education, especially those agreeing with Dr. Coe's[1] conception of the socialized curriculum, should welcome an application of vocational-guidance methods within the church. The adequate manning of the world-wide Christian organization awaits the time when the young people of the Sunday-schools in America shall study and appreciate the religious vocations.

Denominational Enlistment Activities. Denominational colleges and boards of education and special commissions all witness by their concern to the importance of and need for a comprehensive programme. The General Conference of the Methodist Episcopal Church has ordered a commission on life-service. The General Board of Education of the Presbyterian Church in the U. S. A., through its student department, has taken an advance step by inaugurating, in addition to an annual vocational-day programme, a plan for life-work conferences with boys, called "a recruiting measure for the ministry and missions." Boys of high-school age, of promise and character, are gathered by the church session for a one-evening supper-conference. The presence of elders and pastors pleases the boys. Addresses bring home the need for Christian workers, but no expressions or pledges are sought. Through such conferences nearly five thousand boys have already been reached.

III. Some Qualifying Considerations

One must be cautious, however, in attempting to interpret a secular movement which has developed to

---

[1]Coe, G. A., "Social Theory of Religious Education," Scribners, N. Y., 1917. For suggestion to study occupations in Sunday-school curriculum, see p. 105.

deal largely with industrial and commercial callings. From the outset, a clear recognition of certain limitations and modifications must be kept in mind. For the purposes of this survey, religious workers differ from secular workers in at least four particulars.

1. Men in religious vocations never work primarily for money. They work for money, but not for money **primarily**. This is not saying that all other men do. Undoubtedly many men in many callings work from a higher motive than mere financial gain. Where mixed motives are so universally prevalent, money alone is not adequate to account for any man's labor. However, unless the man engaged in full-time, Christian, salaried service **always** places the chief emphasis upon **full-time Christian** rather than upon **salaried,** he ultimately fails. Approximately, it may be said, therefore, that, while other men work to earn a living, he works to spend a life; and this motive in the case of religious workers is indispensable. Every reference in the following pages to salary and to financial advancement must be read with this constantly in mind.

2. In religious vocations work never stops with the whistle. Other men shut the desk, lock the shop, register out, or knock off for the day; but the man in the religious calling does not check out and go home to forget his task. In a certain sense, he follows his calling twenty-four hours every day in the year. In his case it is not so much how many miles he travels, how many letters he writes, how many sermons he preaches, how many calls he makes, or how many conferences he participates in; in short, it is not how many hours he works or what he does, but what he is that counts most. As Mr. Wilson puts it in speaking of the ministry:

"The only profession which consists in being something is the ministry of our Lord and Saviour, and it does not consist of anything else.'" To talk about the conditions of employment or the hours of labor is somewhat beside the point here, because the religious worker, minister, missionary, or layman, can have no eight-hour day.

3. Religious vocations are to a degree one vocation. Even yet they are in a fluid state, blending, and mixing. While this condition prevails less than formerly, it is still much easier to discuss Christian service in terms of function as preaching, teaching, healing, and socializing. The printer stays printer, the plumber and plasterer, though side by side, are always distinguishable; and a man does not ordinarily pass with facility from bricklayer to architect or from chauffeur to civil engineer. With regard to the religious worker, on the other hand, it is easily conceivable that a man, beginning his career as a pastor's assistant and ending it, for example, as a national interdenominational executive, might fill in the course of events any five or six of a dozen vocational positions, withal not losing a moment's time or retracing a single step or in any way breaking the continuity of a useful and successful career. The attempt, therefore, to classify religious vocations is an approximation only, amounting almost to an effort to separate the inseparable.

4. The qualifications for religious workers reduce largely to one qualification. To succeed in the religious callings the only absolutely indispensable quality is love. Traits of personality are important; it is desirable

[1]Wilson, Woodrow, "Minister and the Community," in "Claims and Opportunities of the Christian Ministry," Mott, J. R., Editor, International Commission, Y. M. C. A., 1911, p. 119.

and valuable within limits to analyze and emphasize and point out those characteristics which go best with this or that career; but after invoicing the whole stock of human virtues[1] one finds one's self working in a circle at the centre of which is love. With love any worker, in any field of religious service, may hope to be wonderfully used of God. Even in the area of the industrial and commercial pursuits, vocational guidance hesitates to influence vocational choice by pigeonholing types of personality. How much more must caution be shown in the case of those callings which have in their vocabularly such terms as these: "born again," "greater love * * *," "power of God," and "* * * Christ who strengthened me." The card of admission to the religious workers' guild bears one condition only: the passion to serve.

All these limitations and reservations notwithstanding, vocational guidance offers in this' field a valuable contribution. Misfits and failures do occur in the ministry, in missions, and in the lay work of the church. They will increasingly occur without more adequate vocational information, because the time of specialization and division of labor has reached Christian organizations. Both in the home-field and overseas, positions becoming increasingly differentiated and selective, demand more and.more a careful sorting of candidate material. In the face of the world's opportunity for service and the appeal of the church for fit workers, Christian young people must be not only inspired for service: they must be informed about service as well. Entering religious work, while not less a

---

[1]Coe, G. A., "Virtue and the Virtues," Journal of Religious Education, January, 1912, pp. 485-92.

matter of heart, must become more a matter of head, of sober deliberation and discriminating choice.

Of this age of specialization the tugboat, that industrious bit of marine energy so much in evidence in New York harbor, may be taken as a symbol. Flatboats and barges carry the freight; the tug specializes in power. That is all it carries. When in use it is a fine economizer in the business of sea transportation. Taken alone, it becomes exceedingly useless and wasteful. To count for anything, a tug must be alongside a suitable load, pulling or pushing. This text-book attempts to help Christian young people, already throbbing with His power, to come alongside the right load, where their own aptitudes will find adequate play, ''working with the minimum of friction and the maximum of satisfaction.'''

'Dewey, John, ''Democracy and Education,'' Macmillan and Co., N. Y., 1917, p. 360.

PART I

MINISTER

"Religion has been and is the greatest factor in society because it is the bulwark of the will to carry on."

GIDDINGS.

"A young man of intellectual power may be sure of his fitness for the ministry if his whole heart kindles into flame as he reads and ponders these words: 'Blessed are they that hunger and thirst after righteousness: for they shall be filled.'"

G. A. GORDON.

CHAPTER II

THE PASTOR

An American preacher[1] was talking one day in Paris with Mr. David Lloyd George. He was remarking that had he followed his first intention as a lad in Scotland of entering upon a political career, he might then be among the statesmen gathered at the peace table. For a moment the British premier was pensive, and then soberly replied: "I believe that you have chosen the better part."

Such tributes to the ministry are not uncommon from men of large affairs. In general the disparagement of the pulpit is the small business of petty minds, characteristic of at least three classes of persons: the infidel, the ignoble, and the ignorant. Within the third of these groups must be included, unfortunately, a large number of worthy young people whose unripe judgments, and untamed, over-eager spirit of youth, lead them to accept too readily the estimate of the street, the shop, and the stage that the pulpit is not the place for the red-blooded twentieth-century young man.

The Christian who holds such a view simply lacks information. He is unacquainted with the modern minister, his world message, and his new programme in the changing order of society. The modern clergyman is a real man, of strong personality, wide influence, and

[1]He is too modest to allow the use of his name.

27

great power. He is not at all like the conventional parson of the stage, described by Dr. Cadman,[1] "a character which is in point of manliness and brains the shadow of a shade, glimmering on the verge of downright idiocy." Whatever may be the case as to the present place of the clergy as a class, it is undoubtedly true that the successful, individual clergyman has never stood higher in the affections of his people, in popular respect, and in public leadership.

Nearly two thousand years have passed since Jesus by the sea of Galilee prepared the way for the mustard-seed church. To-day in the United States alone, that portion of the pastors representing Him who bear the name evangelical Protestant have a parish of twenty-five million and more. During these centuries the church and society have developed together. In the lives of individuals, in homes, in schools, in hospitals, in standards, in morals, in marriage vows, in funeral rites, in laws, as well as in ideals the brand of Christ is upon the land. One can about as well imagine one's self in Mars as in America without the church. And yet, however important and useful it has proved in the past, it may serve infinitely more in the present.

This is true because civilization is passing from an industrial into a social age. Now the whole world is a melting-pot of ideas. Self-consciousness, both for individuals and for groups, is more acute than ever before; and it is exactly in this field of exalted personality and of newly-valued human relationships that the church functions, and into which the modern clergyman, no longer held back by an imaginary barrier between the sacred and secular, is prepared whole-heartedly to enter.

---

[1]Cadman, S. Parkes, "Ambassadors of God." Macmillan, N. Y., 1920, p. 137.

The minister to-day has a message for all classes, conditions, races, and nations of men. He alone of all workers occupies a position where he can help both sides to every controversy. His God is the logical mediator between capital and labor, between foreign-born and native, between rich and poor, black and white, Occident and Orient; and, since warriors, politicians, and statesmen fail to disentangle themselves from national greed, prejudice, and hatred, it is the minister, finally, who has the privilege of separating himself long enough and far enough from a national god, to lead out humanity under the great God universal into the plains of peace.

The modern minister is the man at the centre of life. Other men specialize in this thing or that, one in engineering, another in banking, another in medicine, and another in law. All of these are worthy callings, but all of them to a greater or less extent demand the best hours of each day and the best years of each life for the restricted activities of a single compartment of activity. While the lawyer is spending his days delving into annual reports, a slave to technicality and precedent, the minister is majoring in men, in motives, and in the eternal values, touching lives at every point. Rightly conceived, religion is not a separate phase of human endeavor. It embraces the whole of it. To attempt to include religion in a definition is like dipping water with a sieve. To define it takes a volume, and then that volume needs revision every year. Lyman Abbott says religion is God living in the souls of men. The minister, then, is the one who, by making God live through the lives of men, furnishes that morale which is the hope and the power of progress.

Definition and Types of Work. In the present study the term minister is used to include those who are duly authorized to administer the sacraments and to perform all the usual functions of the ministry, of leadership in religious services, or in church life. Many of these are not in actual service as pastors, for ministers are found in every religious vocation. Leaving several of those in which they predominate to be considered in the remainder of this part, the present chapter considers the work of the minister as pastor only. The types of pastorate are many. They vary from the Fifth Avenue parish to the parish of the Tennessee circuit-rider, while in between are all kinds of down-town, neighborhood, village, and open-country parishes, as well as the parishes among student, immigrant, and industrial communities. Keeping this fact of great diversity in mind, there are, generally speaking, at least two main types of pastorate, (1) the urban, and (2) the rural. Before considering the distinctive features of these, however, the programme, difficulties, compensations, and desirable qualities for the pastor in general will be discussed.

Programme. The underlying purpose of the Christian pastor is to promote the Kingdom of God; and his parish is his whole community. In the pulpit, in the study, in the neighborhood, and upon the platform, this is his life work. In the pulpit he preaches the gospel unto the saving of souls. That this is the first item in his varied programme, all pastors apparently agree. In his sermon he embodies elements of the prophet, the priest, and the teacher of sound principles of health, morals, business, politics, and social relations. Keeping himself free from all embarrassing entanglements, he stirs the consciences of his laymen to make the whole world better in all its relationships.

But his programme is one of organization as well as of exhortation. His study becomes the businesslike headquarters of an administrator who manages a great, religious, ethical, and educational organization. Here he plans adequate measures of religious education, here he enlists and encourages leadership for the varied activities of his church. It is to him here that youth come for counsel, and it is from here that he goes into the homes and the hospitals, or to stand by the fresh grave to give comfort to the sorrowing.

In the neighborhood he stands for co-operation, and for the promotion of all community activities, lectures, clubs, and betterment enterprises. He not only takes hold and helps with the plans which others have suggested, but he is always seeking to provide channels for the expression of group-life beyond the limits of his own church membership, for the pastor who has no eye or eagerness for, or influence upon the life outside his own pews belongs to the past.

Nor does the modern clergyman neglect the opportunities of the platform. He attends conventions and conferences, both denominational and interdenominational, his policy being to advance the cause of Christian union and to contribute to the growth of every worthy agency of the church at home and abroad. This does not mean sectarianism. Forty-eight clergymen, representing the seven largest denominations, were asked to rank in importance a list of seven items, containing among others "To promote denominational programmes." Not one placed it first; fourteen scratched it out entirely; and the combined score of the forty-eight questionnaires ranked it at the bottom of the list. There is indeed no place for narrowness or pettiness in the broad, constructive programme of the modern preacher.

Difficulties. Such a man is the first to feel the disadvantage, which exists in most over-churched areas, of duplicating the work of other churches in the community and in the slowing down effect of denominational divisions upon all social undertakings. Sectarianism is felt to be a very real obstacle by many pastors. Even more than the denominational, however, is felt the keen competition from modern complex life. Even the country is not free from this modern absorption in money getting and pleasure seeking. In both city and country evil is organized under many names to attract and to control. Commercialized amusements set a pace for sensationalism and speed which the church would not meet if it could. To the pastor comes a great burden of sorrow-bearing. Sadness and woe he cannot escape, for people in trouble are those whom he first seeks out. In solemn hours at the hospital, in the tragic moment by the death bed, at the open grave, a surprisingly large share of his life is spent; and the continual drain upon his sympathies and his spirits, if he be true shepherd, is simply appalling.

"Lack of response in service and substance from the church membership," is a disappointment which is inevitable for the pastor with a great vision. Whenever a leader is wholly satisfied with those who follow him, it is, perhaps, a sign that he has ceased to lead. This accounts for the constant complaint of the lack of vision on the part of the people; of the indifference of people to the message of the church; of the lack of a sense of responsibility; of the slowness of people to grasp the new idea of the church as the spiritual dynamic of the community; of being able to secure only the fringe of the time of the volunteer workers upon whom one must rely. This continual gap between vision and accomplishment is always a trial to the prophet. He must watch and pray lest the keen edge of his own zeal be gradually worn down. It is not without effort that he maintains at high level his own personal religious life and escapes from the blight of professionalism. Since he works by faith rather than by sight he must guard well the eye of faith, that it grow not dim or blurred.

Yet another disadvantage to the work of the pastor is the lack of business efficiency in the church. Of all the live, working institutions in the world, the church is doubtless the last to be adequately systematized. There are reasons for this which are not hard to find. Spiritual goods are not to be sorted out and arranged in regular rows on shelves, to be invoiced and tagged, and sold, wrapped, and delivered like hardware over the counter. And yet, even so, the pastor faces a multiplicity of duties, exactions on time and strength, which, without organization, lead to waste of time and exhaustion of energy in attention to little things. Without some method, which is usually lacking, for placing first things first, a large task and a splendid opportunity are dissipated through being spread out over too wide a surface. This is to-day one of the most real problems of the minister. Equally applicable to many pastors, America over, is this remark of the private secretary of a busy pastor: "There isn't such a thing in his life as a disengaged moment."

Satisfactions. "Were it possible for the lips of all those who love and revere you as a brother in Christ to sound in your ears the sentiments of their hearts the music of their chorus at this glad hour would be like the noise of many waters.'' These words which voiced upon one occasion the tribute of a grateful church illustrates one of the pastor's compensations. He is the recipient of gratitude abounding. But this is not his chief reward.

The chief joy of the Christian minister is leading souls to salvation. This means something more than simply leading them to an open confession of Christ. It means redeeming and developing character. It means saving and training for the service of society strong religious and ethical personalities. To the pastor as to none other comes the rare privilege of holding up the standards of Jesus Christ and the possibility of shaping life programmes.

The compensation of the prophet's vision and message is his. To influence and guide toward righteous ends every civic interest is his increasing privilege. His power comes not through direct participation, but rather through the indirect permeating presence of a fine spirit, acting as a tonic in the lives of men. In the words of Dr. Finis Idleman, ''it is the church only which sends out those fresh currents which keep business and society clean, and sweetens the springs of life.''

Touching life at the top is a third compensation. Through the consciousness of direct obedience to God in life and in daily purpose the minister lives in the spirit of the upper room, and there he gathers about himself human friendships of rare inspiration. He enjoys association with men and women who are helpful and stimulating, who give and call forth the best. He has a welcome always to the finest Christian home-life. On the other hand, while touching life at the top, he also has the chance to touch it at the very bottom; literally to pull men up out of despair and sin; and his life becomes rich in helpfulness. Through his manifold ministrations to men and his identification of himself with his timeless message, there gradually comes to him the "sense of a kind of earth-immortality through the linking of an individual life with an undying institution, the church," for he works with that which perishes not. "God buries his workers but carries on his work."

The ministry offers another advantage in the opportunity for self-cultivation. A great task develops personality. Human contacts enrich one's life. A full day with a varied programme calls forth personal growth. One who is inspired by a vision of service for God has the highest incentive for making himself as broad and deep a channel as possible. Added to this the pastorate offers a man the greatest personal freedom. He does not know what a time clock is. He regulates his own affairs. To him every hour of study, every new sermon, every additional call in the home may be a stepping-stone to a larger, more effective self. Phillips Brooks said: "The Christian ministry is the largest field for the growth of a human soul that the world affords."

Desirable Qualities. In this section will be considered those natural or acquirable personal qualifications deemed desirable for success in the ministry. Educational qualifications will be considered in a separate section. No attempt will be made here or in similar parts of following chapters to separate these traits into physical, mental, or spiritual; or to determine which of them are innate and which are the result of experience or self-cultivation. Such detailed analysis is not warranted by the purpose in hand, which is merely to sug·

gest in a most general way, and that always with the caution that exceptions and modifications are to be allowed for, the kind of character a person ought to have or to cultivate for the largest usefulness in each calling.

The successful pastor is first of all himself a Christian. That means he is a man who realizes his own sinfulness and reposes all his confidence and hope in his Saviour, Jesus Christ. His love for God and men has made him gentle, forgiving, and true; and has unfolded within him a marvelous sympathy, equipping him with insight, with compassion, and tenderness toward all sorts and conditions of men, women, and children; and has set him on fire with a passion to serve.

To this experience all other qualities are secondary, but they are, nevertheless, important. The pastor is an unconquerable idealist. Henry Clay never could have made a great minister, for he was a great compromiser. The true prophet of God is kind, and patient, and long-suffering, and is able to catch the other man's point of view, but he does not compromise with sin. He keeps one eye on the unseeable and forges ahead in faith. Mr. Beecher told the Yale theological students that in his own ministry the greatest source of help and power had been a temperament "that enabled him to see the unseeable and know the unknowable."[1]

And after faith the minister's greatest prerequisite is hope. "We are saved by hope." There is little enough room for pessimism anywhere, but in the pulpit it is impossible. The preacher must have great confidence in God and in men. He must *know* that things will come out right. He possesses indefatigable hope,

---

[1] Abbott. Lyman, "Henry Ward Beecher," Houghton, Mifflin, N. Y., 1903, p. 128.

tirelessness of spirit, fairly radiating joy and the expectation of the good. The pastor is a man transformed by a definite Christian experience, consumed with a passion to serve, well armored in faith, preaching a gospel of hope; and he is something more. Beecher said he must be a man of imagination, emotion, enthusiasm, and conviction. And still that is not enough.

The man who succeeds in the pastorate is more than a walking catalogue of virtues. He is a personality. Just what makes up and completes that totality it is impossible to say. "He must possess winsomeness and charm of personality, striking contacts immediately." The pastor who said that, himself exemplifies in rare measure the charm and force of personality of which he is speaking. It pervades his conversation, it is the soul of his sermon, it somehow is the unseen thread which knits together his thriving congregation, which has been built up against pressing odds in the heart of Manhattan. Perhaps personality is a matter of growth. If so, there are two elements which the pastor can cultivate to assist in its development. One of these is absolute sincerity, "freedom from cant, and even the suspicion of professionalism."

The other factor is love, free and unhindered love for service and for souls. A pastor was asked to criticize and to add to a list of desirable qualities for the minister. A vacant space was left for his suggestions. After checking the list, he added in the blank as the first requirement for a successful pastor three words: "Love, love, love."

I. CITY PASTOR

Routine. All that has so far been said applies to the ministry in general and to the pastor in particular, in almost any field in which he serves. It is impossible to go further in detail in describing his work and his preparation without selecting a definite type of pastorate as an example. In this case, consider a church with a membership of about eight hundred, in a city of between one hundred and two hundred thousand population, located in the Central West. It must be borne in mind, that even after confining the study in this manner, there is still great variation. What will be the actual schedule of work for such a pastor? It may be assumed that he will prepare eight sermons a month. The preparation of each of these sermons is a large undertaking. It represents first a purpose. That is always the most important thing about a sermon. It therefore is one unit in a definitely thought-out and carefully planned policy or campaign or larger purpose on the part of the minister. Into the sermon he puts his best of scholarship, of newness of thought, and of freshness of illustrative material. After a preacher has stood before the same congregation four Sundays a month for ten months a year for ten or twelve years, sermon-making requires real spade work in deep soil and not simply raking and scratching over the surface of old accumulations.

Just to prepare those eight sermons a month is enough to keep one man fairly busy, but in addition to this work of study, which probably represents at least an average of four hours a day, five days a week, the busy pastor manages to attend about ten special meetings of one kind or another during the month, and to prepare and deliver four extra addresses. This is not to mention eight or ten committee meetings which he also attends. Then there are the calls, of which he averages fifty a month. He has usually about five weddings

during the month, and there is never a week passes
without the gloom of a funeral. Other interruptions
are occurring constantly. Perhaps he teaches a class,
maybe he has personal conferences which take
at least an hour each day, besides correspondence
and office and administrative work amounting to
an hour or two additional. One can readily concur
with the sentiment expressed by Dr. Charles E. Jefferson, when in the course of that delightful "Pastor's
Annual Report,'" he said, "You see, I am an institution on my own hook."

Preparation. The man who hopes to succeed in a
city pastorate should take every advantage for a thorough education. The requirements for ordination, which
vary with different denominations, are not standardized,
and a stated amount of education is rarely a prerequisite.
Men have succeeded in the past and will succeed in the
future in the pastorate by virtue of sheer native ability,
common sense, the Holy Spirit, and the capacity to
make life itself serve them as university. Such men
are exceptions.

The approved standard is a four-year college course
and three-year seminary training, which includes, besides courses in religious education, psychology of religion, comparative religions, and other courses, more
or less elective, the standard studies of theology, exegesis,
history of the church, systematic theology, or the history
and study of Christian doctrine, and practical theology,
which has to do with the science and art of preaching
and carrying on the various functions of the church.
There is a growing tendency to emphasize the study of
psychology, sociology, and economics, especially in con-

---
¹The 23rd.

nection with industrial relations, and to allow the more classical studies such as Greek and Hebrew to become elective. Undoubtedly wide latitude for individual differences and preferences should be and are increasingly allowed. The age at which a man decides to enter the ministry affects the question of preparation. Each man must decide for himself after seeking due advice from the authorities of his own denomination as to the best investment of his time in preparing for service; and all men must realize that Dr. Cadman voices the conviction of this age when he says:[1] "The Christian message must be founded not in the loose rubble of emotional appeal which ministers especially are tempted to use, but upon the solid facts which show one's reverence for the ethics of the intellect."

Statistics.* The more than thirty denominations, "the constituent bodies" of the Federal Council, report no less than 115,000 ministers.[2] Just how these are distributed among the religious vocations is largely a matter of estimate. It is possible only in the most general way, applying as a basis the precentages of distribution found by the government census of 1916,[3] to assume that the number of pastors is about sixty-eight per cent of the total number, or 70,000. This is intended to include all those in exclusively pastoral work, both urban and rural, in the United States.

The pastor's salary is low, but not as ridiculously low as popularly assumed. From 1906 to 1916 the average salary rose from $668 to $1,078.[3] Even this figure is too low, for average salaries by denominations,

[1]Cadman, S. Parkes, "Ambassadors of God," Macmillan, N. Y., 1920, p. 194.
[2]"Yearbook of the Churches," Revell, N. Y., 1920, p. 238.
[3]"Religious Bodies," Bulletin 142, Department of Commerce, Washington, 1920.
*For this and all following sections on statistics, see Appendix 2.

ranging from \$1,166 (Baptists), to \$1,632 (Episcopal),
show an average salary for eight denominations of
\$1,332. For the type of pastorate considered in this
section, upon which a minister enters at about the age
of twenty-six or later, salaries range from \$2,000 in
early years to an average at full maturity of \$5,000.

The Fifth Avenue Church. A study made by the
writer of ten cosmopolitan New York City Protestant
Evangelical churches, including all nine Fifth Avenue
churches and one Broadway church, and representing
five denominations, justifies the following approximate
statements. The average church membership is twelve
hundred; the average length of pastorate, about twenty
years; average age of pastor, about fifty-eight; average
annual salary, \$12,000. One church in four provides,
in addition, a house. These ten churches employ twelve
"junior" or "associate" pastors. The ages at which
these have been called average over thirty-eight;
salaries average \$3,500, but five of the twelve receive
\$4,000 or more.

The Fifth Avenue church is, of course, in many ways
the exception, and Fifth Avenue salaries are unusual.
Yet Fifth Avenue pastors probably have as much difficulty making both ends meet as do their brother ministers in western cities with half their incomes. This illustrates splendidly the fact, which must be taken universally into account with regard to the salaries of the
clergy, that a church board ordinarily endeavors to fit
its pastor's pay to local conditions. Variation is great,
but the successful minister may increasingly anticipate
at the hands of his church a decent living.[1]

---

[1]Account must also be taken of the various systems of old age
pensions or ministerial relief. Funds provided differ among denominations but practically all of them are increasingly providing for su-
perannuated clergymen,

Estimates can only be made as to the opportunities in this vocation. John R. Mott[1] found that between 1895 and 1905 the number of theological students fell off eighteen per cent, although during the same period the membership of the churches increased twenty-six per cent. He states, "I have learned of no denomination in which there is not a demand for more men of ability for the ministry in all sections of the country." The 1920 yearbook of one large denomination reports 2,200 vacant churches. The Christian pastorate offers a wide and attractive and waiting field for the Christian young manhood of America.

II. COUNTRY PASTOR

Programme. The programme of the rural pastor, in addition to most that has already been described, has some features of its own. These grow out of the present situation in the country. The rural church has rapidly declined. For this slump the steady migration cityward, the coming of the automobile, and the inadequate, itinerating preacher are at least partly to blame. Recent investigation found that in some places as low as twenty-five per cent and ten per cent of the resident membership of churches are attending services. In Ohio[2] it was found that of all churches in the country, including those in villages, sixty-six per cent are without resident pastors. Fifty-five hundred out of sixty-six hundred and forty-two are without full-time preaching, and seven hundred and fifty have none at all. The result of such studies is to show that if the church of the country

---

[1]Mott, J. R., "Future Leadership of the Church," Association Press, N. Y., 1909, p. 5.
[2]Gill and Pinchot, "Six Thousand Country Churches," Macmillan, N. Y., 1919, pp. 9-11.

is to live it must develop a new programme, the principal factor of which must be a resident pastor.

The measures proposed to meet this situation provide first of all for scientific surveys of country areas to determine the elements of strength and of weakness, the factors which are making for and those which are making against wholesome, prosperous community and religious life. On the basis of the survey a whole community is designated as a "central parish," to become closely organized through a central church and branch meeting houses, or out-stations, the "centre" as a whole being served by one pastor, who lives permanently in the area served.

The plan, which has been urged by Edwin L. Earp,[1] also includes a method of "federation," whereby in communities where there is only scattered representation of any one denomination, all may unite for economical and effective church work. The keynote of the new movement is the adoption of new methods by the church, of the effort to rally the country people about the church through community activity and community-betterment plans. The church of to-morrow is to remake the country through making its members better farmers and citizens as well as better Christians. In the words of Dr. Warren H. Wilson, this change is to come about, and already is coming about in certain communities, where the pastor "shifts his prayers from the Holy Land of Syria to the Holy Earth of Maryland."

Difficulties. In some respects the drawbacks to the work in the country differ from those in the city. Bad roads and poor schools are an item. The lack of trained

[1] Earp, Edwin L., "The Rural Church Movement," Methodist Book Concern, N. Y., 1914.

leaders for any form of church work is more keenly felt; and one who has had the advantages of the city feels acutely the isolation from centres of privilege, the lack of intellectual companionship, and the narrow social life, as well as the handicap of working among the conservatism and the provincialism which still partially prevail in the country. For the country **pastor** economic stringency is also a vital problem.

Compensations. On the other hand, the new missionary to the country shares in the reconstruction of whole communities, lying fallow for such undertakings. He has the satisfaction of adjusting community life to world movements; and he steps into a position of recognized community leadership. The present popularity of the city cannot blind one to the fact that almost half the population of the United States is still in the country and that, just as heretofore, to train the youth of the country is to train the future leadership of the cities.

Qualities. The successful leader in the new country church movement must have a love for the country and for country people; a community vision and ambition; and a democratic, friendly spirit. He must be a community, rather than a sectarian, Christian.

Preparation. Heretofore the country parish has been merely the vestibule to a city pastorate, the field-work for ministerial students; but the new programme alters all this. To become the successful preacher of an agricultural Christianity, the new pastor needs agricultural training and farming experience more than he needs theology. If he must choose between a seminary course and a course in a college of agriculture, many leaders suggest the latter. Four years in college, and one or two in theology and one or two in agriculture or education are desirable, with at least the experience of two or three summers doing actual farming work.

Routine. Types of country parish vary almost as widely as those of the city. There are village, county-seat, and open-country churches. Consider an open-country parish in an English-speaking community of the Middle West. In the matter of scheduled work, the resident rural pastor has not the heavy strain of the city pastor. He prepares perhaps only one sermon a week for extemporaneous delivery, and one talk; once in two weeks he may be called upon for an address; every three or four weeks to conduct a funeral; and a wedding comes once in about six weeks. His calls average about ten a week. If, in addition to keeping his garden, acting as Scout-master, or taking time to help the Camp-Fire Girls, and conducting now and then chapel exercise in the public school, he is able to devote ten hours a week to study, he is fortunate.

Statistics. The movement for the social-centre church is just beginning. Opportunities are open in every State and almost every county in the Union. Salaries vary widely with an average for the first year of service at about $900, and at maximum efficiency at $1,800 to $2,000. The successful rural pastor, the one who is prepared to work on the modern programme, has the assurance of a permanent and pleasant pastorate.

Women in the Ministry. Women at the present time carry on two types of work in the ministry. Some are ordained pastors of churches. This movement has gone forward slowly but with increasing success. The International Women Preachers' Association held its first meeting in Chicago in 1920. A recent study made by Mary Sumner Boyd[1] shows that in about fifty smaller denominations women are now ordained to the ministry. Among the Baptists and Disciples of Christ women pastors are occasionally met. The actual number of women ministers, however, is very small. During 1920 the Methodist Episcopal General Conference adopted a resolution giving women ecclesiastical equality. The Episcopal, Lutheran, Congregational, and Presbyterian Churches, however, do not yet allow women to preach.

The second type of work which women are doing in the ministry, one in which they have long been eminently successful, is that of pastor's wife. How large a place the wife of a pastor plays in the success of her husband is seldom realized. She shares his plans, his hardships, and his compensations. She helps many times in his overcrowded routine, and in many cases she supplements and balances shortcomings in his character which, without her, might prove disastrous.

"How do you manage to do two men's work in a single day?" Livingstone once inquired of Spurgeon. "You have forgotten that there are two of us," replied the great London pastor, "and the one you see the least of often does the most work."[2]

---

[1] In "The Woman Citizen," December 18, 1920, pp. 794-5.
[2] Conwell, Russell II., "Life of Charles H. Spurgeon," Philadelphia, 1892, p. 235.

CHAPTER III
THE HOME MISSIONARY

In the North American sector, with the division of home missions, the world war for the Christian conquest of mankind has entered its second phase. The first phase was a campaign to advance a line of churches across the continent. These home-mission churches were simply outposts, more or less isolated, meagre and conservative in programme, denominationally minded, struggling for existence. This preliminary establishment of churches was necessary. It was the indispensable first step. The men who manned the enterprise, called home missionaries, were really religious frontiersmen.

The new home mission of the church contemplates a more comprehensive programme than simply possessing the land through the planting of churches. Its aim is nothing less than the Christianizing of the community. The mission of the church is seen to be something more than maintaining life-saving stations to rescue men out of the world-that-is in order to prepare them for the world-to-come. The church must redeem the community and the whole community, and set up here and now a Christian social order.

The theatre of war shifts, to a certain extent, from the sparsely settled West to the overflowing cities. Not outposts but social centres are the order of the day. Service men of a new type are being recruited, called by such names as "social engineer," "special-group expert," and "foreign-speaking pastor."

These new marching orders in the home field are reorganizing and revitalizing the work of the boards. Departments and workers are becoming specialized. City and country are being surveyed and supplied with adequate plans and methods. The community parish, already described, owes its success and support largely to home-mission boards. Cities are adopting programmes of correlation and federation, and are emphasizing industrial relations, social service, and the maintenance of down-town churches, as well as church extension. The modern home missionary is as apt to be a specialist, serving a particular group, as he is to be a general home missionary. The purpose here is to consider several types of workers, usually ministers, and usually laboring under the authority of home-mission boards, whose vocations will not fall within any other chapter of this book.

I. "General" Home Missionary

The home missionary who accepts service beyond the United States or Canada, is for the present purposes, a foreign missionary, and his work will be described in Part ii. The type of worker included here is, therefore, simply a city or country pastor, working under a mission board on the frontier and his programme, in general, is that already considered in chapter ii. To the extent that the church for which he labors becomes independent, this home missionary ceases to be a missionary. In the past, to a very considerable extent, home-missionary work of this general type has been a form of apprenticeship from which men have graduated to higher positions of executive leadership with their boards or into independent pastorates. Nevertheless, within limits the general home missionary represents a distinctive vocation. More than is the case with any other religious worker in the homeland, perhaps, his is a three-in-one job; he has the function of a pastor, the spirit of a foreign missionary, and the programme of a social-religious worker.

Difficulties. To begin with, the home missionary works in a hard field, where financial support is scant, where trained leaders are lacking, and where the church is weak and faltering. The work is exacting and discouraging. In connection with a call for ministers for the frontier, one of the boards makes the significant qualification that they must have persistence enough to stick in spite of difficulties and discouragements, and love enough for Christ to "turn their backs on all inducements to resign for better positions and easier work."

Satisfactions. The chief reward for enduring the hardships of the missionary trench-life comes through the opportunity for community leadership. The home missionary frequently becomes the voice for his town, his advice being sought in civic, social, and political affairs. Rev. Frank L. Moore, secretary for missions of the Congregational Home-Missionary Society, was at one time a home missionary in Cheyenne, Wyoming. Once in a time of discouragement, he confided to Dr. Gunsaulus, who was passing through the city, his misgivings, and remarked that perhaps he should give up his work; and when Dr. Gunsaulus remonstrated with him, assuring him that he "was shaping the affairs of the State," he only smiled doubtfully. But the very next day he had occasion to recall his visitor's statement when the chief justice of the State called to ask his advice on an important matter.

Qualifications and Preparation. Sound health, common sense, splendid optimism, and heroic temperament, these are the qualities in a man for which home-mission boards look. He must possess to an unusual degree the capacity for finding men where they live and adapting himself to them. He must be able to get close to all classes and conditions of people. In preparation he is assumed to have a college and a theological degree, but in this kind of home-missionary work self-sacrificing consecration counts more than college degrees, and will usually find a place waitng for it.

Statistics. Of the four thousand full-time workers employed by the Protestant home-mission boards, probably no less than 1,800 are ordained general home missionaries. The average salary is about $1,500 and manse. The boards are calling for more than six hundred men now.

II. PASTOR TO SPECIAL GROUPS

This field is limitless. There are the lumber camp, the mill town, the Indian, the Negro, the miner, and the immigrant. There are the rural parish, the industrial-centre parish, the city-immigrant parish, the southern-mountain parish, and the downtown-city-church parish. The missionary in these special fields is increasingly a hand-picked man, especially qualified and especially prepared for his task. These specialized vocations, offering permanent life positions, are more and more calling out men of parts and vision. One or two examples only will be considered to illustrate the genius of this phase of the new home-missionary enterprise.

Immigrant Pastor. The Christian minister who is an expert with the immigrant group finds a parish in almost every American city. In the last hundred years thirty or forty million people have passed through America's wide-open, hospitable door. The trouble has been that to most of these Uncle Sam has proved a very poor host, folding his hands and letting them shift for themselves. Speaking in terms of the races of men, New York is the capital of humanity, and there four out of every ten persons are foreign born.

Programme. In New York City, where this kind of work is probably best organized, the immigrant expert has charge of a group of centres, or local churches, each with its own pastor and staff of lay and volunteer workers, together joined in a community parish. One such community leader has in his force four or five ministers, both native and foreign, and twenty-five other paid workers, and perhaps fifty part-time, volunteer helpers. His work is to plan, confer, and execute. In the highest sense he is a supervisor and specialist, knowing the ten-fold fascination of dealing with the human natures of not one class or race of people, but of all classes and of eight or ten races. He is a Christian statesman who has under his thumb all the human problems of the world. He is every day face to face in fact with the problems of Catholicism, of anarchy, of socialism, and of race hatred. He moulds out of chaos Christian character and ethical standards, community neighborliness and brotherhood, which in the area in which he works mean world brotherhood.

Difficulties and Satisfactions. The hard problems in such a programme fall too thick to catalogue. The immigrant worker hurdles an obstacle at every step. He finds half a million people swirled by the centripetal force of circumstance into one small vicinity, a jostling mass of mediocracy. There is no common standard, no common ideal, no common language, no common tradition, no homogeneity, no social consciousness. The social expert has simply five hundred thousand separate pieces of ill-sorted human material out of which to try to build a healthy, wholesome, purposive, accomplishing community. Trouble enough in that! No wonder that he must absorb himself in the slums; no wonder that he is shut off from outside interests; no wonder that he finds the work taxing and so demanding that he is apt to fray himself out in bootless scattering of activities and in anxiety and worry.

Satisfactions. The rewards are the professional pride of any engineer who plans and achieves a great work which the world needs, with the added satisfaction which comes to him as a social engineer that he has wrought in the hardest field, the slum, with the rawest material, the immigrant, for the highest purpose, the bringing in of the democracy of God.

Preparation. In addition to a college and seminary course the worker in this field of specialization needs to have had much preliminary experience through volunteer service. Provision is made by some schools for students to do summer field-work under supervision. Most of all the specialist needs first-hand knowledge of the peoples among whom he is to work. To this end, more than one mission board now provides scholarships for choice men to spend at least one year abroad at the various sources of immigration, studying the language, literature, and lives of the people.

Foreign-Speaking Pastor. This type of minister is required in the home-mission enterprise for pastoral work among adult immigrants. The children soon learn English in the schools, but in spite of the goal that all immigrants should adopt not only American ideals and standards but also the language of America, parents cling to their native tongue. If immigration should cease, there would be no need for this worker after fifteen or twenty years, but in the meantime he is indispensable.

Foreign-speaking pastors are of three kinds: Foreign-born, native-born of foreign parents, and native-born of native parents. Those of the first kind are liable to be deficient in English and in comprehending fully the Christian message; those of the third kind are liable to be deficient in understanding the foreign language and point of view. All things considered, if he has had good educational advantages, the man of the second type embodies the advantages of the first and third without the disadvantages of either. There are perhaps a dozen colleges in the United States which now offer special arrangements for training these men, in some the provision being for a four-year college and theological course, open to those with a grade-school education, in others, for a three-year college and theological course for those having at least high-school training.

Student Pastor. At many university and educational centres denominational pastors are employed who take as their parish the whole student body, with its numbers of thinking students facing problems of readjustment. This is a fairly new form of work which does not come strictly under home-mission auspices. It is not considered a home-mission enterprise. It is more closely related to the denominational boards of education, or indeed, may be carried on wholly under a strong local church, or in connection with a student Y. M. C. A.

The denominational pastor makes it his business to know personally all students, who come from homes of similar faith, to know them by their first names, or maybe by their nicknames. He holds conferences with them in his office, helping them to iron out such difficulties as failure in scholarship, or moral breakdown. In times of illness he visits them; and in the conduct of funerals and marriage services he is to the student body a regular pastor. Through his intimacy with the students, which extends so far as to include entertaining them in his own home, he is a strong asset in all the work of the local church. He conducts classes, promotes the young people's society, plans student parties and receptions at the church, and is always at the door at Sunday services, greeting the students and enlarging his acquaintance with them.

A man develops into such a place of vital service as this through pastoral experience extending through some years. He must be a thorough scholar, a man of insight, and a man who is more than a good mixer. He must be a best mixer. For a background he must have a rich college experience of his own and he must be sympathetic and enthusiastic and familiar with the interests and activities of college men, able to enter wholeheartedly into the full life of the campus. Rev.

H. M. Moore, in writing abount his experience of seven years at Ithaca, among Cornell students, concludes with the statement: "I never had in the years of my ministry anything which brought the satisfaction that this work did."

Statistics. Today the Protestant home-mission boards are probably employing no less than seven hundred or eight hundred ministers in the various forms of specialized service. Salaries vary from $1,800 and manse to $6,000.

CHAPTER IV

TWO SPECIALISTS

I. Chaplain

The chaplain specializes in soldiers. The life of the soldier is ordinarily as monotonous in peace as it is thrilling in war. After returning to be showered with gratitude, the conquering hero who remains in the service settles down to a thankless grind of discipline and routine. The popularity of the army and navy in time of fighting is only equalled by their unpopularity at other times. Yet in peace as well as in war the men in uniform are on duty for the republic. Big-hearted, stalwart, and physically-fit men they are who live under abnormal conditions, without the customary moral support of home and social environment.

Programme. Whether in army or navy, the chaplain is an ordained minister who dons the uniform and accepts the regiment or the ship as his parish. His sermons to the men are usually of the short, practical kind. His best sermons are his life and example of Christian friendship. In addition to having charge of all religious services, attendance upon which is voluntary and which he conducts according to the practice of the denomination to which he belongs, he also promotes Sunday-school, holiday services, special

56

attractions, and recreational and educational activities. He visits all the sick, as well as the men under arrest. Marriages, funerals, baptisms, and other pastoral work come within his province. Although a pastor, his conduct, no less than that of the fighting men, is governed by specific regulations.

Difficulties. Perhaps the chief problem of the chaplain is to avoid getting into the deadly rut of army life. He lacks stimulating outside contacts; and, being left largely to his own devices, he has a temptation, as Gaylord S. White[1] suggests, to procrastinate and to become mentally and spiritually stagnant. With the possible exception of the financial, he has all the problems of the regular pastor, and he has them in an intensified degree. Especially in the navy, he has the added handicap of long absences from his family, for each three-year period of land service is usually alternated with a three-year cruise, during which time only occasional and brief shore-leave is possible.

Compensations. Whatever troubles he may have, the chaplain never has to complain, as some ministers do, of a lack of men in his parish. He has about him every hour of every day the challenge of bringing Christ home to men, and to men whose need for Christian spirit, Christian standards, and Christian motives, is doubly great. Military prestige is perhaps an attraction, for from the first the chaplain ranks as an officer. His pay is certain and promotion assured. Patriotic considerations are present also. He serves his country as directly as he serves his God, for he contributes

---

[1] From an ''Outline of a Proposed Course on the Chaplaincy of the Army and Navy for Theological Seminaries.''

largely to that morale which is always the soul of the military establishment.

Qualifications. No candidate is accepted as a chaplain without passing a fairly severe physical examination. He must be reasonably sound in every respect. Beyond this, he should possess "dignity and a democratic spirit," tact, and adaptability. He must have none of the chameleon about him. He must stand firm and not be swayed to and fro by every wind that blows. As Rev. E. O. Watson[1] expresses it, "He must be a real man, and a man's man."

Preparation. A regular college and theological course is recommended although not absolutely prescribed for the chaplain. In the examination which is given for army chaplain candidates, the most weight attaches to "pastoral work as clergyman." Second in importance stands "attendance at college."[2] Every candidate must be an ordained minister, a member in good standing of the denomination to which he belongs, must be recommended by some ecclesiastical body, and must be between the ages of twenty-three and forty-five. In the navy he must be between twenty-one and thirty-one and a half.

Promotion. In the army, the chaplain enters as lieutenant, being promoted at the end of five years to captain, at the end of fourteen to major, and at the end of twenty to lieutenant-colonel. As lieutenant his salary is $2,500 a year. In addition, if he is married, he

[1]Secretary of the General Commission of Army and Navy Chaplains, to whose kindness the writer is indebted for the facts of this section.
[2]"Appointment of Chaplains in the U. S. Army," Washington, 1918, Special Bulletin No. 3, pp. 8-9.

is assigned suitable quarters. At maximum rank, that of lieutenant-colonel, he receives between $5,000 and $6,000. In the navy, the chaplain enters as a junior-grade lieutenant, being promoted after seven years to lieutenant, and, after four more years, to lieutenant-commander. Beyond this, promotion is by selection, the highest rank being that of captain, which corresponds to a colonel in the army. The pay in the navy is practically equivalent to that in the army.

Statistics. In the army are about 105 regular chaplains, of whom seventy-three per cent are Protestant; in the navy, about 108, of whom seventy-eight per cent are Protestant.[1] This is, however, on a peace footing. Since there is approximately one chaplain for each 1,200 officers and men, the opportunities for recruits in this form of religious vocation increase at the rate of about eighty for each hundred thousand men called to the colors.

II. EVANGELIST

The evangelist is assumed to be a specialist in conversion. For the purposes of this book, he may be defined as a minister who devotes himself exclusively to conducting revivals, protracted meetings, or evangelistic services for churches or groups of churches. Although many times regular pastors, by carrying on such meetings either in their own or neighboring churches, assume for the time being the role of evangelist, the present section undertakes to treat only of the professional in this field.

---

[1]"Yearbook of the Churches," Revell, N. Y., 1920, pp. 181-5.

Programme. While in general his programme differs little from that of the pastor, there are respects in which the evangelist's work is more or less specialized. In the first place, he lays special stress upon the winning of souls. He drives home to the sinner the simple sound doctrine of salvation by repentance and regeneration through the Spirit of God. He is conservative and thoroughly orthodox in doctrine, emphatic and convincing in method. In this connection, he encourages Bible study and personal soul-winning among the church members, for personal work is the keynote of his message.

But the evangelist is more than a converter. He not only plans to increase the membership of the church but to revitalize it as well. He discusses popular sins which the pastor too often fails to tackle; he raises deficits or increases church budgets and stimulates Christian stewardship; he frequently launches building campaigns; he gives a new impetus to gospel singing; he recruits volunteers for religious life-service; he inaugurates new and better methods in local congregations. Advancing the cause of Christian union may be set down as a feature of his programme, especially if his meeting is a co-operative effort among several churches. In short, to a greater extent than is popularly understood, the evangelist is one who comes to set things in order.

The Meeting. Revival meetings are of two types, single-church and union. If a well-known evangelist is called to hold a meeting in a middle-western city of one to two hundred thousand population, six times out of ten it is a meeting of the union type, in which perhaps six or eight churches unite. Such a meeting is likely to last about six weeks, have an average attendance of 1,200, and result in something like 450 accessions by confession, 100 by letter, and 150 by reinstatement. If it is a one-church meeting, it is likely to last about three weeks, with an average attendance of about 500, and result in 150 accessions by confession, and forty each by letter and reinstatement. All such estimates as these are subject to great variation.

Routine. The successful evangelist holds from seven to nine meetings a year, spending perhaps eight months in the field. His routine, for whichever type of meeting he holds, is about the same. In the course of a week he gives ten sermons, four addresses, and five or six talks. In addition to half a dozen conferences, four or five noon meetings, and two or three special-group gatherings, he conducts ten regular services. Crowded in between talking and meeting people in crowds, the evangelist manages to make fifteen or twenty calls and hold thirty or forty interviews. Study is usually crowded down to about ten hours a week.

Difficulties. A majority of the twenty evangelists interrogated by the writer consider their greatest problem to be "working against adverse local conditions." Added to the general indifference, which is the great hindrance to revivals, they find all sorts of special troubles which need ironing out. Perhaps the congregation is divided, or the pastor is unpopular; or spirituality is at a low ebb; or the church is going on financial rocks. The evangelist never faces ideal conditions. He cannot expect to. It is usually because there is something wrong that he is sent for. The case here is somewhat analogous to having a physician say that his greatest problem is finding his patients sick!

However, there are other difficulties as well. Of these, absence from one's family for a greater share of the time is not the least. Bad weather during meetings is an annoyance which must be cheerfully and frequently endured. Organizing the lay forces of the church for effective service is a slow and trying task for a man who comes into the community a virtual stranger and who finds a tendency on the part of the people to let him do the work. Sectarianism is frequently mentioned as a hindrance by those engaged in holding union meetings.

What is probably the most vital drawback to the work of the evangelist remains to be considered. There is a widespread and growing sentiment among the church at large which is unfavorable to the professional evangelist. "Being accused of being a grafter and fleecer," which several evangelists mention as one of the problems, is one form in which this sentiment finds expression. The injudicious methods of some evangelists, which have operated to bring discredit upon all; the apparent lack of permanence of results; and the impossibility of adopting a method and subject-matter which will find acceptance with all classes of people, saints and sinners, intellectuals and emotionals, at the same time, are among the factors which are to blame for this condition.

Among the contributory causes which are at work beneath the surface should be included the notion that gradual education rather than sudden conversion is the normal course of religious development. A recent study[1] of revivals seems to indicate that possibly "the effect of the revivals is not to increase the total conversions" (Coe) but merely to hasten them, thus making accession a matter of spurt rather than of steady increase, which would come without them. Possibly the net gain of the revival is more apparent than real. Then, again, the current socializing of the Christian message appears to favor a new conception of social conversion, which shall take into account not only the individual seeking salvation but the community and group interests, activities, and ideals through which personal salvation must be wrought. This point of view is illustrated by the following quotation from Paul Moore Strayer, inserted here wholly for the purpose of indicating one of the chief problems which faces the evangelist:

"His (the evangelist's) training does not fit him to lead in the great movement for social readjustment. His message does not stir the social conscience and deepen the sense of civic responsibility in those he gets together, and the revival method has almost collapsed."[2]

Satisfactions. Whatever may be, in the light of such criticisms, the desirable readjustment in evangelistic methods and standards, the evangelist has the assurance that his message and purpose are vital to the church. "Adding unto the church" will remain a fundamental item of its programme as long as the church endures; and the evangelist finds his great charter in the Acts of the Apostles.

---

[1]Dike, Samuel W., "A Study of New England Revivals," American Journal of Sociology, Vol. XV, 1909, pp. 361-78.
[2]"The Reconstruction of the Church," Macmillan, N. Y., 1919, p. 203.

The need for some form of evangelistic effort is pressing. Whereas the churches grew sixty-one per cent from 1890 to 1906, in the next ten years they increased only nineteen per cent.[1] From these figures it is possible to estimate that in the year 1890 there was one addition to the church for each twenty-seven members; but in the year 1916, it required sixty-eight Christians to win one. In one large denomination in a recent year one thousand churches reported no additions by confession. It is such a condition as this among the churches of the land which accounts for the fact that the evangelist finds one source of compensation in the conviction that his work is the greatest possible opportunity in this generation for serving Christ and the church.

The chief compensation of the evangelist is to preach the gospel to multitudes who are hungry for the bread of life, who are eager for the old story in all its direct force and power. Among these are many who never otherwise hear a sermon. These it is the unique privilege of the evangelist to reach, for, in addition to reviving the church and putting it to work, and to opening the eyes of the people to a new sense of sin and responsibility, the evangelist has the sure knowledge that he stimulates church attendance and popularizes the church in the community.

Desirable Qualities. It is not possible to set off a distinct set of qualities which fit the evangelist in contrast to those which are desirable for the minister in general. Certain qualifications are, however, relatively important. The evangelist must possess not only a

---

[1]Bulletin 142, Department of Commerce, Bureau of Census, Washington, 1920, p. 29.

religious experience which has made him love God, but he must to a marked degree be a lover of men as well. His must be a magnetic, powerful-to-persuade, dead-in-earnest personality. To a strong physique, good control of temper, discretion, and keen sense of humor, he should add a manly appearance of dignity and poise.

Preparation. Ministers do not ordinarily step out of the seminary into successful evangelistic work. At least five years of regular pastoral experience and responsibility seems a desirable apprenticeship for the evangelist. Some successful evangelists suggest a course in a Bible college in preference to the regular theological training, which, however, remains the normal standard.

Statistics. Accurate figures are nowhere available for this vocation. The membership list of the Interdenominational Association of Evangelists[1] for 1919-20 includes 208 "accredited and authorized evangelists." A very conservative estimate, no doubt, would be five hundred professional Protestant evangelists. Men usually enter this distinctive field of service at about thirty-five. In his first years, the evangelist gets about $2,000 annually. In his prime, his salary ranges all the way from $3,600 to $10,000, with an average at about $5,000.

---

[1]General Secretary, Winona Lake, Indiana.

CHAPTER V

THE "MAN HIGHER UP"

Beside the vocations of pastor, general home missionary, specialized home missionary, chaplain, and evangelist, the ordained minister has open to him, in addition to many others, at least three types of position These are religious editor, religious educator, and denominational and interdenominational executive. None of these places are pre-empted by clergymen, but clergymen probably predominate in them. None of them are ordinarily open to newly ordained men. They are recruited primarily by selection from the ranks of the pastorate. They represent the highest vocational promotion within the gift of the church. By the term "man higher up" is meant simply this: that in the scheme of organized religious enterprise such a one occupies a place nearer the apex of the pyramid.

I. RELIGIOUS EDITOR

Dr. Henry H. Myers estimates the total circulation for religious literature in the United States at thirty to thirty-five million: an audience fit to challenge the best output of a Christian press. To meet this market, publications of all types in large quantities are prepared. The publication societies of the denominational boards, representing an outlay of nearly half a million dollars annually, employ many workers, some of them

66

young people with journalistic ability who are working up. Many others, laymen and clergy, contribute from time to time, but are not wholly identified with editorial work. The chief executive, in the main, is an ordained minister.

Programme. The religious editor supervises and directs a staff, representing perhaps five departments: teachers', young people's, elementary, foreign-language and missionary literature, and home publications, all producing text-books, quarterlies, promotional material, and periodicals. The editor is responsible for general policies and standards. He writes and edits, but he also inspires the writing of others.

Other Considerations. "There are no chief problems, but a swarm of minor ones coming up each day," writes Amos R. Wells of the work of the religous editor. As to desirable qualities, these are broad scholarship, wide sympathy, the spirit of enterprise, imagination, vision, constructive-mindedness, and, above all, literary power. The college and theological training which, as minister, this worker may be assumed to possess, should include, especially if the editor of the future is to meet the demands of the new religious education, considerable specialization in literature, and rather less of theology and more of pedagogy.

Statistics. At least thirty-two donominations now have Sunday-school departments employing editors. In addition, there are about two hundred donominational publications, eighty per cent of which are edited by clergymen. Three hundred would be a low estimate for the ordained ministers engaged solely in work as religious editors. Salaries range from $2,500 at time of appointment to $6,000 at maximum efficiency.

II. RELIGIOUS EDUCATOR

Evangelical Protestant schools, colleges, and seminaries in the United States number no less than 1,200, with more than a quarter of a million students. Practically one hundred per cent of the faculties of the theological seminaries, and twenty per cent to thirty per cent of all other denominational schools are ministers. Perhaps ninety-five per cent of the presidents of denominational colleges are clergymen. Many are directors of religious education, also. (See Part III, Chapter XIII.) Ministers fill the positions of instructors, professors, heads and deans of departments, and presidents.

Programme. The programme of the religious educator is that of any educator plus religious teaching and direct Christian influence. Most ordained men preach more or less regularly in connection with school work. Teaching for the clergyman has both advantages and disadvantages. "There are plenty of both," as Dean Vichert expresses it. If the teacher is a successful public speaker, who has once felt the fascination of preaching, he is apt to grow restless under the restrictions and limitations of teaching. Dr. Hugh Black points out that the teacher has the problem to avoid becoming static and academic and removed from real life.

On the other hand, the college or seminary professor, teaching and developing a religious subject in which he is deeply concerned, released from pastoral cares and responsibilities, free from ecclesiastical or political pressure of any kind, as he usually is, cultivating the peculiarly significant relationship which exists only between scholar and teacher, enjoys a rare opportunity for genuine personal satisfaction and far-reaching influence. Not his least compensation is to live in what John L. Seaton calls "an atmosphere in which the passion for service easily grows."

Qualifications and Preparation. The kind of man wanted by institutions of religious education possesses a passion for his subject and thorough knowledge of it, deep sympathy with youth, the capacity to command the respect and confidence of the students, an attractive and inspiring personality, a scholarly mind, Christian idealism, and a gift for teaching, qualities easily catalogued but with great difficulty assembled in one human being. College degrees come much easier. Of these the least that is acceptable to-day is an A. M. for teaching in college, and for teaching in seminaries, four years in college, a seminary course, and two or three additional years of graduate study, evidenced by the degree of Ph. D.

Statistics. Probably no less than 2,000 ministers are employed in full-time religious teaching and administrative work. Salaries vary greatly, depending upon type and size of school, and upon position. Men are seldom called under thirty, and the salary at first ranges from $1,500 to $2,000; at maximum, from $3,000 to $4,500.

III. THE EXECUTIVE

Not all the men of big business are in industry. Much of the highest-keyed, most alert man-power in America is linked up with the Christian church, which is no mean enterprise. Organized departments of church work in the United States handle more money and employ more men than many harvester companies, automobile concerns, national banks, hotels, factories, and mills. One foreign-mission board alone collects and disburses annually more than $7,000,000, another $3,000,000, and one woman's board, $2,000,000. The combined home and foreign missionary undertaking of the Protestant church represents not less than $43,-000,000 annually and a total full-time payroll of not less than 15,000 workers. Just the administrative "overhead" (salaries, rents, etc.) of the home-mission boards alone represents three-quarters of a million annually.

In New York City, where the headquarters for many of the denominations and for much interdenominational work are located, the national executives of Christianity take on the spirit of the great cosmopolitan city. The whir, the virility, the power of the metropolis get into their blood. In skyscraper offices above the roar of the streets, overlooking the world, with secretaries and ante-rooms, where typewriters continually buzz, these men appear right certainly men of large affairs, confident, polished, poised, sure of themselves, low-speaking, incisive, intense, capable and cordial, the effective higher servants of the Kingdom of God, which in this generation has become a great, going, thriving, spiritual concern.

Types. The small army of executives who head church and interchurch programmes may roughly be classified as (1) general national executives, or "senior secretaries," (2) departmental secretaries, or "directors," and (3) field executives, or "missionary superintendents." These last are usually regional executives, administering over a State, synod, or district. It is not always easy to draw clear distinctions either between these three types, or between these purely executive positions with those which call for field promotional work, which is considered in chapter xi. Practically all the executives considered here are clergymen, Along with other departments or boards of the church, such as home, foreign, education, publication, Sunday-school, church-extension, there are ususally women's boards, especially of home and foreign missions. The executives of these boards are women, to whom in general what is said here applies equally.

Programme. The general programme of an executive depends entirely upon the phase of the work with which he is attached. If he is with the foreign board, he carries in head and heart the responsibility for initiating and promoting policies and plans, for getting the home church behind the foreign undertaking. The programme, difficulties, and satisfactions of the foreign missionary himself are, to a certain extent, his. If he is employed as a secretary of the Federal Council of the Churches of Christ in America, the outstanding, most tangible object lesson in the world of Christ's prayer that they all might be one, his work also varies with the particular commission with which he is associated.

Routine. In any of these positions it is impossible to schedule a man's work. It is not unusual for him to send out as many as a thousand letters a month. He spends his days at headquarters, in interviews and a regular round of nerve-and-brain-consuming conferences with leaders. Perhaps he delivers as many as ten addresses a month or more, and a fifth of his time probably he spends in travel.

Difficulties. Such work, therefore, involves considerable absence from home, night-work, and the wear and tear of travel. It goes without saying that the secretaryship means financial loss and the giving up of business and personal success in other lines. The requirement for unusual gifts is so high that no one can succeed here who could not succeed in other places of leadership. In one board is a man to-day who gave up a salary of three times what he now gets. Another problem is the fact that the executive is more or less cut off from personal contacts with the body of the church. Some men feel this so keenly that they ask to be relieved from successful work in order to get back to the enrichening relationships of parish life.

The greatest drawback to this type of worker, however, is the inherent difficulty in attempting to lead a great organization which is to its core democratic. In other kinds of management, where the same standards of efficiency prevail, the chief executive is an autocrat, who controls absolutely. In the Protestant church there is no autocracy, men's opinions differ, and their adherence to a plan must be won, not commanded. The organization is a democracy; the president, an unseen lord. Thus every world-vision which the executive by virtue of his position at the central office comes to cherish is all too slow of accomplishment.

Satisfactions. Compensations come to the executive in proportion to the privilege given him of putting his life into big plans, of promoting unity in spirit and action, and in seeing Christianity move splendidly forward across the world. His position gives him an enlarged point of view, a widened acquaintanceship and fellowship with men of rare endowments; and through his organized activities and country-wide contacts he multiplies his life many times in influence.

Qualifications. Good judgment, ability to inspire confidence and to meet people, and especially an "interchurch attitude of mind," is Dr. Roy Guild's description of a fit man for the interdenominational secretaryship. A level head and administrative and platform ability are desirable. Such a man is a forceful personality, with a well-developed capacity for co-operation. Dr. Robert E. Speer writes that the secretary should possess the qualities which one would look for in a faithful and efficient man anywhere, "plus more than ordinary executive ability and more than ordinary capacity to state a case or make an appeal."

Preparation. The usual preparation for the executive is a successful pastorate. A man is often called for a position for which his past conspicuous success especially fits him. In other cases he is promoted from the position of regional to that of national executive, or from that of departmental or associate secretary. He is seldom if ever called directly from the seminary.

Statistics. On the basis of the government census for 1916, which indicated that about two per cent of ministers were engaged in non-pastoral denominational work, it may be assumed that not less than 2,000 clergymen are to-day filling such positions as those here described. Regional executives enter the field about the age of thirty, salary $2,000 to $4,000; directors, probably called somewhat later, salary $4,000 to $5,000; and national denominational board executives called at an average age of about forty-five, $6,000 to $8,000.

This completes the survey of those distinctive types of occupations in which the minister in the United States ordinarily serves. It is not exhaustive. Some types of work to which entrance is selective have been included even though not of direct concern for the recruit in order to indicate the rich variety and significance of the ministry, which to-day affords abundant opportunity for young men, twenty-five to forty-five, preferably married, who possess, in the words of Grant K. Lewis, "a big faculty of common sense, and who are in harmony with the spirit of the age."

REFERENCES

PART I

GENERAL

a. Crawford, Leonidas W., "Vocations within the Church," Abingdon Press, New York City, 1920.
b. Diffendorfer, Ralph E., "Church and the Community," Interchurch, New York City, 1920.
c. Strayer, Paul M., "Reconstruction of the Church," Macmillan, New York City, 1919.
d. "Yearbook of the Churches," Federal Council of Churches of Christ in America, New York City, 1920.

CHAPTER I

e. Allen, Frederick J., "Source Book of Occupations," Harvard University Press, 1921.
f. Brewer, John M., "Vocational Guidance Movement," Macmillan, New York City, 1919.

CHAPTER II

g. Abbott, Lyman, "Christian Ministry," Houghton Mifflin Co., New York City, 1905.
h. Cadman, S. Parkes, "Ambassadors of God," Macmillan, New York City, 1920.
i. Mott, John R., "Future Leadership of the Church," Associated Press, New York City, 1909.
j. Mott, John R., "Claims and Opportunities of the Christian Ministry," Do., 1919.
k. Morse, Richard, "Fear God in Your Own Community," Henry Holt and Co., New York City, 1918.
l. Wilson, Lucius E., "Community Leadership: the New Profession," American City Bureau, New York City, 1919.
m. Hoyt, Arthur S., "The Preacher," Macmillan Co., New York City, 1909.

Chapter III

n. Douglass, H. Paul, "The New Home Missions," Missionary Education Movement, New York City, 1914.

o. McClure, Archibald, "Leadership of the New America," George H. Doran Co., New York City, 1916.

p. Whittles, Thomas D., "Frank Higgins, Trail Blazer," Interchurch World Movement, New York City, 1920.

Chapter IV

q. Cavert, Samuel McC., "Church's Distinguished-Service Cross," in "The Continent," November 6, 1919.

r. Coe, Geo. A., "Psychology of Religion," University of Chicago Press, 1916.

s. Frazier, John B., "Navy Chaplain's Manual," Federal Council of Churches of Christ in America, New York City, 1918.

t. Ottman, Ford C., "Life of J. Wilbur Chapman," Doubleday, Page and Co., New York City, 1920.

u. Stearns, Gustav, "From Army Camps and Battlefields," Augsburg Publishing Company, Minneapolis, Minn., 1920.

Chapter V

v. Guild, Roy B., "Community Programs for Co-operating Churches," Chapter IX, Associated Press, New York City, 1920.

ASSIGNMENTS

PART I

CHAPTER I

* What constitutes a call to religious work?
* Which of these three factors should have most weight in determining one's choice of life-work: (1) need, (2) fitness, (3) ''call''?
* To what extent should financial remuneration influence a religious worker's choice of a vocation?
1. Prepare a chart showing the various church and interchurch organizations from smallest local unit to highest international relationships (see a, d, and the yearbook of your own denomination), indicate vocational openings.

CHAPTER II

* What is the source of the granting of special privileges to the clergy? Should they continue to be granted?
* Who was the most successful pastor you have known? What was the secret of his success?
2. Contrast the urban and rural pastor in as many points as possible.
3. Describe at least five different types of parish (see b).
4. Explain how a rural church can develop its resources in order to serve best the whole community (see k).

CHAPTER III

* In what respects does a home missionary differ from a foreign missionary?
* What home-missionary work have you ever done or seen done?
5. Describe the work of the home missionary in a logging camp (see p).
6. Tell about other groups in the United States, Jew, Oriental, Mormon, who require home-missionary work.

CHAPTER IV

* When are the services of a chaplain more needed by the men to whom he is assigned, in war or in peace?

7. If the army should be raised to 1,200,000 men, how many chaplains would be required?

8. Read the life of an evangelist, reporting to the class the vocational steps in his career, early decision, preparation, qualities, success.

CHAPTER V

9. Tell the class about the work and programme of one of your denominational boards.

IN GENERAL

* Was Jesus ordained? Humanly speaking, was He pastor, missionary, evangelist, teacher? Classify His activities vocationally.

10. Interview a worker in one of the vocations described in this section, aiming in your report to bring out additional points.

11. Which vocation presented is most desirable? Which least desirable?

12. Study case 2 (appendix 4) and be prepared to advise the subject of it, case 5, case 8.

13. Select the chief difficulty and the chief desirable quality which are most nearly distinctive of each type of worker considered.

14. For a special project for part 1, see appendix 3.

PART II

FOREIGN MISSIONARY

"Almost any man or woman with a well-poised mind in a sound body, with a living Christian character and an intense desire to have other men share his faith and knowledge, can be utilized on the vast plantation of the mission field."

GALEN M. FISHER.

79

"There are women 'pouring tea' all winter who might be lifting hundreds of Oriental girls into new womanhood. There are able-bodied Americans without a vision or a task, useless as chips on the stream, when they might be directing the main currents of life for a province or a nation. Devotion to a great cause makes a great life."

PRESIDENT FAUNCE.

CHAPTER VI

GENERAL ORDAINED MISSIONARY

I. Ordained Evangelist

"I want to go to that part of the world where men seem to be most lost," said a man, afterward Bishop of Uganda. That part of the world, many think, is to be found in the field of foreign missions. It is there where hospitals and doctors are most scarce, where schools are most rare, where social welfare has least meaning, and where enlightenment awaits longest the transforming power of a knowledge of Jesus Christ.

For each ten thousand of population Africa has only fifty-three Christian communicants, India, only eighteen, Japan, only fourteen, and China, only eight. Cut out a paper disc about the size of a silver dollar. Stick through it at the centre an ordinary flat-headed pin. Let the disc represent the population of Japan, and the head of the pin indicates approximately Japan's entire Christian community. The areas still unoccupied by Protestant missions in Asia, Africa, and South America about equal in extent and in population the North American continent. In a group of one hundred, representing the population of the world, Christians, including those of the Roman Catholic and Eastern churches, holding the adherence of only thirty-six, will be outnumbered by heathen religionists almost two to one. In some places the Christian missionary has not gone, in others he has only a foothold, in others he fights with his heels dug in; everywhere he advances against odds and nowhere is he yet victorious.

Programme. In the face of this world situation, Christianity mobilizes its forces. However, although an ever-increasing division of labor brings not only physicians and nurses, but teachers, agriculturists, social workers, and other specialists into the enterprise, the general missionary, the ordained preacher of the gospel, continues to bear in large measure the brunt of the Christian conquest of the world. His is a clear-cut programme. It is none other than the Great Commission—old, yet new with each generation—to go, to make disciples of all the nations, and always to look confidently to Jesus Christ for His presence, His guidance, and His power.

In carrying out this universal programme, the work of the general missionary divides into several types, one of which is pioneering. The pioneer attacks new fields. He is a scout for Christianity and for civilization who plunges alone into the unexplored to make a clearing in the hearts of a wilderness people for the church, the school, and the hospital. The apostle to the Lao, Dr. McGilvray, was such a pioneer. Once, on a trip of exploration, he caught the trail of a people of strange tongue. He followed them. He established among them the first church where now there are a score of churches with a membership of 4,000. He laid the foundations of a medical work which now consists of five hospitals, and of an educational work now numbering eight boarding and twenty-two elementary schools. Christian pioneering is not yet finished. In East Siam alone are four provinces with a population of 2,500,000* awaiting the voice of one crying in the wilderness, make ye ready the way of the Lord.

The pioneer may in the course of time carry on other types of work. The general missionary may, indeed, fill any one of several positions. He may be pastor of a large church, director of an institutional church, superintendent of city or district evangelistic work, perhaps a professor in or president of a theological school. He may serve in more than one capacity at once. The type of his work differs also with the field in which he is engaged.

African Rural Mission. In a rural mission in Africa, for example, he has a varied schedule. He preaches regularly. He goes frequently on tour, holding evangelistic meetings and inspecting out-stations. In the meantime he oversees the whole work of the station, church, school, and hospital; and trains and directs native forces. Perhaps he prepares literature. He deals with backsliders. He is moral physician to the community as well as to his flock; arbiter of differences between Christians; friend and advisor to chiefs and rulers. He must know how to do everything from digging a well to sewing on buttons or designing dresses for women; from cultivating friendships, gardening, cobbling, binding a book, mending furniture, running a magic lantern, and managing the print-shop, to performing the rites of the undertaker. During every hour of every busy day of overseeing, encouraging, inspiring, preaching, and instructing, he is

*Speer, R. E., "Student Volunteer Movement Bulletin," January, 1921, p. 15.

engaged in the constant activity of personal soul-winning and of living a Christlike life before men, which is the core of the missionary's task.

District Superintendent in China. A different picture is that of a district superintendent of a well-organized area in China. Within a radius of perhaps fifty miles this missionary worker may have under his care twenty churches, some in villages with a membership of thirty to two hundred, where there will be also an elementary mission school for girls and one for boys; some in larger towns or cities with a membership as high as 1,200, as completely organized as churches at the home base, and each of them probably carrying on a volunteer evangelistic work through small chapels and street meetings which put to shame many American churches. Chinese pastors serve all these churches. The work of the superintendent is to make a round of his district from one to three times a year, to conduct special evangelistic meetings here and there, and to conduct annual conferences or institutes, lasting about ten days, for the training and inspiring of his Chinese pastors, for he is in very real way the spiritual father of the pastors, churches, and workers of his district.

Difficulties. The man who becomes a general missionary, whatever be his specific task, faces ceaseless activity, hard work, and heavy responsibility. Room enough here for romance and heroism! Yet in the presence of many pressing problems his sense of the romantic soon wears off. The first difficulties are those of adjustment. The native language tests him severely. "Here a man lays hold on something as difficult as a whole college course, with nothing but grammars, dictionaries, and the grace of God to help him.''* For the most of the first year and perhaps the second this task absorbs him. Hardly less difficult is his adjustment to the climate. From it he has no escape. Night and day it is hunting weak spots in his constitution. From the deadly rays of the sun he must shield himself; from the sudden chill after sunset he must wrap himself; and against the insidious malaria he must continually drug himself.

To native society he must also get adjusted. Not all natives are degraded, filthy, and repulsive, but some are; and the missionary confronts the acute problem of transforming the general concept of Christ's boundless love and of universal brotherhood into concrete personal contacts with people from which he would naturally shrink. Finally he faces another adjustment as hard as the language, and as dangerous as the climate —adjustment to the loneliness in which he finds himself. Home, classmates, friends, are wiped out of his immediate life. He is no longer one among a great association, sharing common institutions, traditions, and aspirations under a common flag and with a common civilzation. He is like a man in a lighthouse far off shore, in a far-off sea, left alone. To many this proves the most severe trial of missionary life.

The difficulties of the work itself are great. The missionary's church is itself isolated. In programmes for personal and social righteousness it stands comparatively alone, supported by no public opinion not of its own creating. As plans for social and community betterment enlarge, the brunt of building sentiment and

---

*Peeke, Rev. H. V. S., in ''Call, Qualifications, and Preparation of Missionary Candidates,'' Student Volunteer Movement, 1906, p. 201.

of inspiring social organizations falls upon the single-handed church, and the load of the missionary is increased. International relations present another delicate problem. Although his interests are primarily religious, the position of the missionary as leader of a great vital force for civilization places his work peculiarly at the mercy of the shifting relations between nations. Almost daily he faces the astute questioning of native scholars, many of them men of high attainment, keen of intellect, and sound in logic, who are often learned not only in native religions but who are surprisingly familiar with Christianity itself, especially with the points of attack made upon it in the homeland by scholars of modern scientific method.

The frailty and shortcomings of the native converts, whose conduct so often leaves much to be desired, is apt to be a sore trial to the missionary, who must learn to be long-suffering with people just emerging from generations of sin and immorality, people who still find about them the quicksand of the old life waiting on every side to draw them under again. Although the missionary labors and prays incessantly in the midst of fields white unto the harvest, the tangible garnering of human souls proceeds so slowly that the missionary must realize with Dr. Luther Gulick that "winning the world is a campaign, not a skirmish."

Some of the most trying personal problems of the missionary remain to be considered. His domestic life is one. The missionary shares his marriage plans with his mission board, for wives are missionaries, too, and their credentials are very properly looked into. Furthermore, raising a family on the mission field almost inevitably means eventually a separation from chil dren, and perhaps from wife as well, when the time for American schooling comes. Work in a foreign mission has other drawbacks. One is that distance from the base of supplies, in connection with the shortage of workers which practically always prevails, makes emergencies caused by illness, death, removal, or furlough always a serious concern, to the sudden effects of which one's plans are always exposed. A second is the increased health risk. Of the deaths among missionaries since 1890, sixty per cent* have been victims of so-called preventable diseases against which they would have been largely shielded at home. A third handicap to life at the missionary front is found in the enforced intimacy of the members of the staff. One must get along with others day in and day out. Like a man quarantined in a boarding house, the missionary finds himself inseparably linked with people not of his own choosing. Finally the missionary by the very nature of his position as a leader, and as the representative of a civilization higher than that among which he lives, confronts various personal temptations. A "dogmatic assertiveness" is apt to creep into his makeup; formalism and professionalism must be guarded against; and he faces a tremendous, incessant pressure toward the lowering of his high standard to the point of becoming spiritually indolent and slothful.

The lot of the missionary is indeed hard. There is no harder task. No man should undertake it without counting the cost, without realizing the frightful strain, physical, mental, and spiritual, which confronts him, and which in a relatively few years overseas is apt to

---

*Findings of the Medical Conference of the World Missionary Conference, Edinburgh, 1910, reprinted by Lambuth, Walter R., in "Medical Missions," Student Volunteer Movement, New York City, 1920, p. 230.

make of him a veteran of the cross, and always makes of him the supreme example of Christian heroism.

Satisfactions. The path of the foreign missionary is beset with obstacles; but alongside of every obstacle he finds compensation, for in religious work satisfactions always vary directly with difficulties; the greater the difficulty the higher the satisfaction. His work, therefore, is not only hardest but happiest.

The real joys of the missionary, however, cannot be adequately expressed with pen, ink, and paper, and simple declarative sentences, and a one, two, three order. The written page cannot hold them. To labor in a wide field unhampered by sectarianism is worth something; freely to offer oneself and to be accepted and gradually to be built into the very structure of the life of a people, an essential part of its progress, is worth more; to know and to have verified every day the fact that one's life work is placed at the heart of the need of the world, is to thrill with the life abundant. To clothe where men are most naked, to feed where men are most hungry, to teach where men are most ignorant, to sit by the side of men most hopelessly ill in spirit and soul and to nurse them into spiritual health until they grow strong and rise up and go forth and in their turn become angels of light, to be the channel through which God's unspeakable gifts are brought into the lives of individuals and communities, redeeming them with life and love,—this is satisfaction beyond comparison.

The pages of missionary biography, if they be read well between the lines, abound in the compensations and joys of the missionary. We recall Dr. Albert L.

Shelton, that veteran of Tibet, who was captured and held for ransom for many, many days. Although desperately ill he had been heartlessly dragged about from hiding-place to hiding-place until finally he was abandoned by his captors to die. He chanced to be found by a Christian official. The official knew of Dr. Shelton's work. Having gained strength, with the aid of this man, Dr. Shelton started for the coast. In every village he found people who knew of him and his work. The news of his liberation went before him. He came to Christian villages with which he had no personal acquaintance, but where he learned that daily for many weeks prayers had gone up for his safety. As the weary, footsore missionary hurried on he met whole villages which had come out en masse to greet him with tears of rejoicing and hymns of praise. Nearing the coast he met another heart-glad group, including representatives of governments and rulers; and, as the daily press flashed out the message, these shared with thousands of Christians the world around the good news of his safe deliverance. When he reached America, and on every occasion of his appearance since, he has received the respect and love of grateful Christians anxious to shower upon him marks of their esteem.

Truly such tributes, in which all foreign missionaries share, while only feeble forerunners of the higher commendation of conscience which God surely grants to the good and faithful servant, must bring to the missionary soldier, home from overseas, genuine satisfaction and joy.

Desirable Qualities. Grace, grit, and gumption, plus health enough for an insurance policy, and brains enough for a college diploma, are, according to Dr. Jacob Chamberlain of India, the essential personal qualifications for the foreign missionary. The amplification of this topic under the threefold head of physical, mental, and spiritual qualities is also suggested by some one else* when he proposes that the missionary must have "a hard head, a soft heart, and a tough skin."

In addition to sound health, which is imperative, a steady nerve, fearlessness, and common everyday physical courage are still not out of place at the missionary front. Decision, complete self-control, boundless energy, and an unquenchable spirit of enterprise and youthful venturesomeness which never grows old, are invaluable. An acceptable trio are political sagacity, fine tact, and good judgment; while broadmindedness and a scientific spirit, which cultivate the scholarly habits of modesty, caution, accuracy, observation, and inductive method, are increasingly an asset. Indispensable for the general missionary is that elusive, perhaps inborn quality, probably the resultant of many blended traits, called leadership.

Of desirable spiritual qualities an unshakable faith in God, in Jesus, in the Holy Spirit, in the Bible, and in prayer stands first. The mission field has no room for a doubting man, "for a missionary ceases to be a missionary as soon as he doubts that he has a message that is eternal." Catholicity, sympathy, idealism, and a spirit of full surrender to and dependence upon God are all of great worth in the missionary; but the two qualities most essential are, first, such a passion

*Report on Preparation of Educational Missionaries, Board of Missionary Preparation, New York City, 1917, p. 75.
[1]De Forest, Rev. J. H., in "Call, Qualifications, and Preparation of Missionary Candidates," Student Volunteer Movement, 1906, p. 113.

for preaching as would lead its possessor to agree with
John Scudder of India who, when his eyesight began
to fail, could say, "I would sooner lose my eyesight
than my voice;"[1] and, second, that subtle fragrance
of the great Christian soul, called spirituality, which
not only keeps him sweet and fresh and winsome and
strong, but permeates all the atmosphere round about
him with peace and confidence. A missionary's ultimate effectiveness and power depend upon a spiritual
endurance which enables him to live on and not famish
in the heat and dust and scorching wind of the desert,
having within him rivers of living water. Spirituality
must be supreme. "Without it missionary work will
be a wearisome grind; with it, it will be liberty and
the joy of a great service."[*]

Preparation. When Jane Thompson wrote from
Kolhapur, "I am so glad God sent me to India," she
unconsciously illustrated, in her recognition of God's
guiding hand, the first essential in the preparation of
the foreign missionary. No one is prepared for overseas missionary service until God has come into his
life in such a real sense as to be sincerely felt to be his
actual leader. The habit of every day acknowledging
God's plan and guidance in every detail of one's life
should be early formed. The mission board says to
the candidate: "Know God!"—and know him intimately in such a way as to have learned to take Him
at His word. For this, no amount of college credit, no
accumulation of missionary data, no reading of missionary biography, however extensive, can take the

---

[1]Franklin, James H., "Ministers of Mercy," Missionary Education
Movement, 1919, p. 237.
[*]Speer, R. E., in "Call, Qualifications, and Preparation of Mis-
sionary Candidates," Student Volunteer Movement, 1906, p. 186.

place. The missionary, it has been said, is, like the poet, born, not made; yes, born again.

The second command of the mission board is: "Know thy Bible!" It is to be read and reread; marked and remarked; learned and relearned; pondered and prayed over, and pondered and prayed over again. Educational psychologists these days are using the term "over-learning" to describe the wasteful situation in school work where, in the course of certain complex exercises, pupils spend more time and drill on some one feature of a process than is required for its comparative learning. Not so with the Bible. For foreign missionary service, the Bible cannot be over-learned.

"Know books!" is the third command of the candidate secretary, by which is meant a broad college education, a requirement which the varied work of the missionary and the comprehensive programme of modern missions amply justify, for both the enterprise and the non-Christian world which it embraces grow increasingly complex. While every course offered in a modern college might conceivably find use in the hands of the missionary worker, especial value attaches to the study of natural science, languages, history, philosophy, sociology, comparative religions, international law, economics, psychology, and hygiene. All this in addition to the later more mature study of Christian theology, which most mission boards consider essential for the general ordained missionary.

Yet one more requirement must the candidate face: "Know the science of missions in general and the problems of your own field in particular!" This means that both in school and out of school, through independent study, the missionary candidate should acquaint himself with the history, methods, and policies of the Christian missionary undertaking, and that he should absorb all that he can about the geography, history, literature, traditions, religions, and present needs of the people to whom he expects to be sent. Beyond the four years in high school, this preparation represents four years in college and at least three years in the theological seminary. The present recommendation, presented by the Board of Missionary Preparation,* provides for a fourth year in the theological seminary, or college of missions, or university centre, for the completion of special missionary training as desirable in general for the ordained missionary. The general ordained missionary, representing probably the broadest, most comprehensive vocation in the whole range of Christian service, requires the most comprehensive, thoroughgoing preparation.

Statistics.† The total foreign staff in the non-Christian world and Latin America is 10,474.¹ Of these men, ordained and unordained, number 4,122. Ordained men alone number 2,803. The distribution of the foreign staff on the basis of the occupations presented in this part is not available. How many less than this last number of ordained missionaries are engaged in general evangelistic work cannot be estimated. The age at which missionaries go out varies greatly, as does also the length of service. In a study of age-distribu-

---

*Report of a Conference on the Preparation of Ordained Missionaries, held in New York, December, 1914, Board of Missionary Preparation, New York, N. Y., pp. 51, 52.
†See Appendix 2.
¹"Foreign Missions Year Book of North America, 1920," Foreign Missions Conference of North America, New York.

tion of 1,101 missionaries on the field, five are found to be twenty-one years old, and two, seventy-seven; the largest number at any age are fifty-six at the age of thirty-two, while the medium age is thirty-six. As to length of service, a study of 1,000 ex-missionaries shows that thirty-nine per cent of those engaged in evangelistic work remained for five years or less. Yet only five in one hundred positions are vacated a year, a five per cent "labor turnover."

Salaries. Salary allowances vary greatly among boards and for different countries. Missionaries everywhere receive a meagre competence, nothing more. The Protestant board which carries on the largest foreign work pays married missionaries in India and most of China a basic salary of $1,300, in Central and South Africa, $1,400, in Europe, Japan, Korea, $1,500, the corresponding salaries for single missionaries being $900, $950, and $1,000. In maintaining separate establishments, single missionaries receive $100 additional. Married missionaries receive a salary increase after five years of $100, and $200 more after ten years, with an added $100 after twenty-five years. Salary increase for single missionaries is one-half that of married missionaries.

An allowance of $100 is made for each child up to and including the age of five; $150, six—fourteen; $200, fifteen—twenty-one, with $50 a year extra when the child is in college in the United States. While on furlough married missionaries receive $1,300, single missionaries, $850, and the stated increases and allowances with, in addition, up to $30 a month for rent, if necessary. Upon retirement, missionaries of this board

are cared for like retired ministers and widows of ministers. These figures[1] may be taken to indicate something of the financial compensations of all regular
missionaries, in whatever type of work engaged.

Calls.[2]   At one time the evangelical Protestant
boards of foreign missions were calling for no less than
454 ordained general missionaries. Other calls will be
indicated at the close of each chapter.

II. Woman Evangelist

Two things all Hindoos are said to agree upon are
"the sanctity of the cow and the depravity of woman;" and half the women of the British Empire are
Hindoo![*]   Forty million women in India are confined
in zenanas. Of twenty-six million widows, 335,000
are under fifteen, more than a hundred thousand, under
ten. The case of India may be accepted in general as
typical of the treatment of women in non-Christian
lands. Only Christianity offers womanhood respect,
freedom, and enlightenment; yet half a billion women
and girls are still beyond the influence of the Christian
church. This situation, because of the barriers of
Oriental custom, affords a special challenge to the
woman missionary.

Programme. Woman's work for woman on the mission field is hardly less varied than the work of the
man. Aside from the woman physician, the nurse, and
the teacher, to be considered later, the field of service

---

[1]Taken from "Field News Letter," Methodist Episcopal Board of
Foreign Missions, September, 1920.
[2]Taken from the "Student Volunteer Movement Bulletin," January,
1921.
[*]Robinson, Charles Henry, "History of Christian Missions,"
Charles Scribner's Sons, New York, 1915, p. 39.

is great, particularly in India and the Moslem lands. As in the case of the man, the work of the woman may combine different types at once, and it differs with localities and countries. As an example, consider the work of a single woman engaged in general evangelistic work in western India. She may be attached to a station situated in a city of perhaps 20,000 population, which has on its compound two schools, an orphanage, and a hospital; and a staff consisting of nine or ten foreign workers, including a woman physician, a nurse, three single women teachers, and two men and their wives. She works in an area with a radius of perhaps fifty miles and with a population of 750,000. In addition to supervising the work of five village day-schools for girls, which she visits once or twice every month, she conducts open-air evangelistic meetings among the women of her district and calls upon the women of the zenanas.

In all her work the woman missionary of this type depends much upon her Bible woman, an Indian, perhaps wife of an Indian pastor, herself a tried and true Christian with an eloquent, straightforward message for her sisters of India. In the course of a month, these two, going usually alone, may visit thirty different villages, each, however, cut by caste groups into five or six hamlets, sometimes several miles apart. In the same time they make sixty or eighty zenana calls. Journeys away from the station for a month or longer are sometimes made, such long tours affording the workers the opportunity of witnessing for Jesus in villages where no missionary has ever been before.

Day's Work. A day's programme would include a start before sunrise, for in India the middle-of-the-day sun must be avoided. Arriving by ox-cart at their destination, the two workers pitch their tent, establishing a headquarters for the day. Within a radius of perhaps five miles they will work. They enter a hamlet to seek an opportunity, wherever one or two will listen, to tell the Christian story. Probably they stop at the public well, for here come women of the village to draw water. Several pause to catch the song which the Bible woman starts. Others gather about, placing their jars of water on the ground. Probably a woman yonder is combing her hair; another here is washing her babe; but what matter! for here are a score of women; and the eager evangelist, who has come to tell of the gift of God, and to give living water, seizes the opportunity, and tells with glowing face of Him who also once spoke to a woman by the well, saying, "Whosoever shall drink of the water that I shall give him shall never thirst; but * (it) * * shall become in him a well of water springing up into eternal life."*

After this service among the untouchables, and one or two of a similar nature in different hamlets, with singing, Scripture reading, and testimony from both workers, they may call at the door of a zenana. Sometimes they are greeted with the unwelcome words, "You are not wanted here; we have our own religion as well as you." More often, however, they are cordially received, especially in those communities where they are acquainted and where the influence of a mission school has made itself felt. More than likely they are asked inside, or they may remain standing in the courtyard before the door. In either event the singing

*John 4:14.

soon attracts the neighbors, who in Oriental style flock in without ceremony. This first call may last thirty or forty minutes, and through it acquaintances are made and the way is opened for later visits. Thus the word is scattered among the women of the shadowed zenana as well as among the women at the well and in the street. By sundown the evangelist and her helper, having made probably five calls and spoken to individuals and groups in five or six hamlets, turn homeward in the confidence that the word shall not return void.

Difficulties. In the main the woman missionary faces the same difficulties as the man. It may be that her responsibility is usually less, and that the burden of the undertaking in the large, therefore, does not bear so heavily upon her. On the other hand, because she is less rugged and robust and because she has a tendency to plunge conscientiously into her work beyond the limit of her strength, climate, fatigue, and anxiety may prove to her especially trying. Moreover, the depressing influence of sin and degradation, the pitifully slow results, the deadening monotony, the exile from the congenial social life of home, all these bear doubly hard upon the sensitive woman.

Satisfactions. Yet for her, too, compensations are forever saving the day. If it is true that woman lives to serve, then she is most happy when she feels herself most needed; and at the missionary front evidences of great need are never absent. If the lot of heathen men is bad, the lot of heathen women is worse. If the men are worth pioneering and fighting and dying for, then who better than Christian woman appreciates the worth to God and to humanity of a woman's soul? It is the motherhood of a Christian nation that-is-to-be which the woman missionary holds in her hand. At her knee she gathers heart-hungry little waifs of the Orient whose clinging small fists find a way to her maternal love; while she finds an answering love which is its own reward when she throws the mantle of hope and life about eager girls and women, like that Indian woman who testified before an audience, saying, "I was a dead woman in my sins, but thanks to God, He has brought me again into life."

Desirable Qualities. The desirable qualifications for the man fit the woman missionary, too. A true woman, full of love, gentle-voiced, refined, tactful, winning, and of dependable cheerfulness, is wanted for missionary service in non-Christian lands. A strong physique and the ability to live and work with others are of prime importance. Her preparation should consist of a full college course, with psychology, sociology, education, history, sciences, languages, English, or general literature, perhaps, as a major. A full course in a normal school or teachers' college would be considered an equivalent. In addition she should have at least one year for special missionary preparation, including such studies as the science and history of missions and the religions of the world; and a thorough course in the Bible. Both groups of studies are offered by several mission colleges and seminaries. The reason for setting a high requirement is because to a large extent the work of the woman missionary is still very composite on the field, demanding broad and thorough preparation. However, the standards here as in all cases vary with needs, with fields contemplated, and with the age and experience of candidates. In large degree every application to a mission board is treated as an individual matter, and decided upon its own merits.

Statistics. The number of unmarried women engaged in all forms of missionary work overseas and in Latin America as we write is 2,978. For general evangelistic work the total calls of the boards for foreign missions for women are 342.

The total number of missionaries' wives, themselves considered missionaries, is 3,372. All these figures, of course, change with the years.

III. MISSIONARY HOME-MAKER

The missionary wife may fill many positions. If on the field before marriage, she may afterward find herself eventually, whatever be her husband's work, continuing more or less as evangelist, physician, teacher, matron, or nurse. Dr. Christine Iverson, who went out to Arabia a single woman, married Dr. Arthur Bennett; and the two doctors, continuing their work, shared their labors side by side and together gave their lives.[1] If as bride she first goes to the field, in addition to her home she will gradually fit into other forms of service, sharing to that extent in the programme and routine, difficulties and joys, common to other workers. The particular work of the married woman missionary,[2] deserving especial mention, however, is that of Christian home-making.

---

[1] Franklin, James H., "Ministers of Mercy," Missionary Education Movement, 1919, Chapter 2.

[2] Occasionally, a mother, also, paying her own expenses, goes with son or daughter to the field, as in the case of Mrs. Pennell, Op. cit., p. 3.

Programme. Against the dark background of immorality, polygamy, degradation of woman, and neglect of children, which the non-Christian world presents, stands out the Christian home as a supreme missionary agency. Not only is the missionary bungalow, presided over by the wife, a refuge where the life of the mission compound with its chapel, kindergarten, school, and hospital activities centres for rest, renewal of strength, and inspiration; and not only is it many times a nest where splendid recruits for the missionary enterprise are reared; but it is also a home-making laboratory where native neighbors come to learn, an experiment station for propagating wholesome, strong, family life around the earth.

Routine. The routine of the composite vocation of home-making is familiar; but, in the case of the Christian home-maker overseas, to such a list of activities as those suggested by Dr. Snedden[1]: the buying, preparing and serving of food, the buying, repairing and making of clothes, household care and upkeep, laundry, care of children, accounting, sick nursing, housing and furnishing, adult sociability, and care of garden, in themselves offering increased problems in foreign lands, must be added the husbanding of an always-slender income, keeping perpetual open house for weary missionaries, and, frequently, the tutoring of one's own children[2] in preparation for their coming to the high school and college in the homeland. This varied and essential occupation is one to tax to the uttermost one's resources of physical strength, of ma-

---

[1]Snedden, D., "Vocational Education," Macmillan Company, New York City, p. 240.

[2]"Preparation of Women for Foreign Missionary Service," Board of Missionary Preparation, New York City, p. 10.

nagerial ability, and of true, womanly, Christian character.

Preparation. A broad college education and special training in such subjects as education, home-making, social service, and first aid cannot come amiss for the missionary married woman. However, calls to foreign service come many times on short notice. In such cases, a missionary spirit, a sense of responsibility, and an appreciation of her opportunity in the missionary programme will help her make up for the lack of a college degree by a wise use of the last months before sailing. On the field her first duty is to learn the language. Such a price is cheap to pay for the privilege which is to be hers. Next to the example of the crucified Lover of Men, the world needs most to have set before it a pattern of Christian home-life, for humanity will never be Christian until it is cradled in Christian homes.

CHAPTER VII

MEDICAL MISSIONARY AND NURSE

I PHYSICIAN

In the fight for the Orient the medical missionary has rendered distinguished service. In hard and in far places, bristling with hostility and suspicion, he has established Christian outposts, and by living in spirit the life of the Great Physician has conquered the good will of wide areas and prepared the way for church and school. The annals of medical missions show that in the advance in the East the Christian physician has indeed many times proved to be for Christianity the passport and defence.

It is the world's appalling need for physical healing which has made the Western doctor so effective an agent in the missionary enterprise. Without him, whole non-Christian populations, devastated by pestilence, fever, and tuberculosis, with countless blind, deformed, insane, and lepers, are wholly at the mercy of a hopelessly incompetent heathen practitioner, who, without knowledge of anatomy, of bone-setting, of antiseptic treatment, of contagion, of bacteriology, of anæsthetics, of hygiene, of nursing and dieting, without even a proper conception of cause and effect, is powerless to prevent endless suffering and the dying of people like flies.

No wonder that the Western physician has made his

way in the East, and that even Moslems and Hindoos
have learned to respect and love him. Yet to-day a
hundred million are still living in territory unoccupied
by medical missions; while China, where the medical
work is well advanced, has six hundred thousand people
to every medical missionary.*

Programme. The Christian doctor attempts a double
cure: the healing of body and the healing of soul. He
is as truly a missionary in spirit and in ultimate purpose as is the ordained evangelist. He is frequently
an ordained man. In his relation to the mission he is
considered a regular missionary, in full sympathy with
and sharing in the responsibility of the whole Christian
enterprise. If evangelistic workers are not available
to visit the wards and to conduct daily services in the
hospital, as well as to carry out follow-up work with
the patients, he himself plans for religious services, including a short service of Scripture reading, testimony,
and prayer at the opening of each day's work. The
Great Commission is inscribed no less on the corner-
stone of the mission hospital than of the mission chapel.

Routine. However, while in principle the medical
missionary is first missionary and second medical, in
practice the medicine comes first. He does not preach,
he heals; and instead of pews he faces packed wards
and an overflow congregation of the afflicted every day
of the year. His actual round of work consists in
diagnosing, treating, and operating. Set in a radius
of perhaps a hundred miles, his hospital provides upwards of a hundred beds and maintains two or three

---

*Lambuth, Walter R., "Medical Missions," Student Volunteer
Movement, New York City, 1920, p. 174.

dispensaries. In addition to a foreign-missionary nurse in charge of the hospital, he has a small native staff of helpers. With this equipment he may care for two thousand in-patients and forty thousand out-patients annually. In one day he may be called upon to treat or operate upon a hundred to two hundred cases. In addition, he administers the affairs of the hospital and dispensaries; and, since it is the settled policy to train up as rapidly as possible native physicians and nurses, he may, besides supervising and instructing his own staff of students and internes, be called upon to teach in a medical school, if one is conveniently located. It may be said in general that in every mission station of the world the medical missionary's opportunity for service is limited only by the hours of the day and his own endurance.

One day a poor blind fellow by a simple operation has his sight restored; and the next week he returns to the hospital leading half a dozen other blind men. For miles and miles around, without regard to age, condition, or creed, the people come. When the physician sometimes goes ajourneying to bring help to those who cannot come to him, he is certain to find everywhere those eager to testify to help and care received at the hospital. If his trip requires haste he seeks to avoid villages on the way, for every chance recognition, every pause by the road, may mean for him hours of delay, mired in a throng of human sufferers. If a great artist should paint a picture entitled, "The Christian Physician at Work," no matter what country or what season or what time of day its setting, the most appropriate words to place beneath it would be these of Mark: "At even when the sun did set they brought unto Him all that were sick and them that were possessed with demons. *And all the city was gathered together at the door.''*

Difficulties. The medical missionary shares all the problems of the general missionary with emphasis upon two. One, which grows out of the limitless opportunity, has to do with the effective conservation of missionary energy. Place a strong man or woman with a sincere ideal of service, willing to be spent, in a field of endless need and the result is apt to be overwork. That has been the result in medical missions. The three words most frequently met with in the closing chapters of the lives of the ministers of mercy are exhaustion—fever—early death. The other special trial for the Christian doctor is the slowness of spiritual results. After all, his chief task is an operation on the heart of his patients which shall transform lives. It is for this he endures hardships and spends so lavishly his youth, his strength, his blood.

People so susceptible to the spread of disease and sin should respond quickly to the contagion of a life vividly and unmistakably Christian. But they do not. One reads in twenty pages a sketch of the stirring life of Theodore Leighton Pennell. The time from this missionary's first arrival in India to his last triumphal march to Bannu is compressed into twenty minutes of reading; but that twenty minutes of reading represents twenty years of grind and grim endeavor, of being misunderstood and misrepresented. That blinded Afghan who came saying, "O, Sahib, if you can give me some sight long enough to go and shoot my enemy,

*Mark 1:32, 33.

then I shall be satisfied to be blind all the rest of my life,'"* may be taken as an example of the spirit pervading all too many who come for aid, the awful deadness of whose souls causes the physician anxiety, heartache, and a continual gnawing consciousness of insufficiency.

Satisfactions. In many cases the M. D. of the medical missionary has meant, Devoted unto Martyrdom; and in every case it means Doer of Mercy. It is in making this a true translation of his title that the missionary physician finds his satisfaction. He has a joyous confidence in ultimate success because he knows that downright unselfish service in love for mankind cannot fail. After twenty-five years in Turkey, Dr. Fred Douglas Shepard said: "I came to bear witness to this, that God is love. And if, by my work or life, I have been able to show this to you, I have had my reward, and for it I thank God.'"

A second compensation comes through the opportunities which his work as a physician gives for personal contacts with men. He does not deal with men en masse, but singly and under circumstances of intimacy and confidence. The preacher must travel from place to place to catch up with men, but the physician in one day at the hospital treats men who come from east, west, north, and south for miles and miles. Thus he becomes the most effective influence for permeating the whole country with Christian ideas and ideals.

Finally, the Christian doctor in the Orient finds himself by virtue of his knowledge and his proved integrity able to penetrate to a greater extent than any other

---

*Franklin, James H., "Ministers of Mercy," Missionary Education Movement, New York City, 1919, p. 5.
¹Op. Cit., p. 5.

missionary worker all barriers of caste and position, to win the respect and confidence of poor and rich, weak and powerful alike, and to become a leader of the people, a counsellor of rulers, a Christian statesman, and an international force. Not only has he transformed the spiritual lives of individuals by his ministry of love but he has been instrumental in shaping the policies of nations as well.

The conversation[1] overheard between two rickshaw men in Nanking sometime ago, when Dr. Macklin, a veteran medical missionary, passed by, registers in a dozen words the place and the compensations of the medical missionary.

"Who is that old gentleman?"

"Don't you know him?"

"No."

"Why, that is Jesus Christ."

Desirable Qualities and Preparation. The missionary qualities to be especially emphasized in the case of the medical missionary are, besides robust health and absence of latent tendencies to physical or mental weakness, resourcefulness, wholesome optimism, level-headedness, true humility, administrative ability, dignified geniality, and genuine sympathy. He must prepare thoroughly, taking in addition to a college course of four years (in exceptional cases two years), four years' medical training, followed by at least one year postgraduate work in a general hospital.[2] He must go to the field well grounded in all that forms the basis of successful practice, medical and surgical. He must

[1] Sloan, T. Dwight, "Medical Advance Guard," Student Volunteer Movement, New York City, p. 9.

[2] "Qualifications and Preparation of Medical Missionaries and Nurses," Board of Missionary Preparation, reprint, New York, 1918.

be familiar with laboratory technique. Diseases of the tropics he needs to study, and the disorders of the skin and eyes. He should qualify in psychopathy and even in dentistry and in filling prescriptions. It is very desirable for him to have a good knowledge of preventive medicine, hygiene, and sanitation. The final step in the candidate's preparation should be the passing of an examination given by State or other authority. In short, for overseas service, the physician requires better and more comprehensive preparation than for practice at home.

Statistics. Medical missionaries number now no less than 389 men and 168 women. In the study of a thousand missionaries above referred to, forty-eight per cent of the physicians were found to have served five years or less. The boards are calling as we write for no less than two hundred men physicians and surgeons and seventeen specialists; and for forty-seven women physicians.

II Nurse

The missionary nurse is essential to the success of the missionary physician. Her work is more humble but hardly less helpful; and the world's need for doctors signifies a world's need for nurses, especially when one is considering lands where, as in China, even a word for "nurse" is unknown.[1]

Programme. The nurse overseas engages in several kinds of work. She may be called upon to serve as visiting nurse, helping to guard communities from epi-

---

[1]Powell, Alice M., "Nurse in the Mission Field," Student Volunteer Movement, New York City, p. 6.

demic, teaching hygiene and dietetics to the women of a neighborhood, or to do district, rural, school, or factory nursing, or to supervise the dispensary of a hospital, or to act as X-ray or laboratory assistant, or to serve as anæsthetist. More and more, however, the primary duty of the American nurse is to act as hospital superintendent and to train and supervise native nurses. To whatever country she goes, and to whatever field, the profession offers her challenging opportunities for original, significant work.

Difficulties. That missionary work is not a romance but a daily routine is probably most acutely realized by the nurse. Her responsibilities are unusually heavy and her annoyances unusually plentiful. The native nurses whom she is training and upon whom she must rely are wofully ignorant and slow to comprehend right medical methods, proving often unreliable. The people themselves, having no idea of hygiene, medicine, and care of the body, make exceedingly poor patients, taking internally external remedies, drinking in one gulp medicine intended to be taken in drops, and clandestinely eating all manner of outlandish things when they are, as likely as not, on a milk diet. The conscientious nurse is kept under a continual strain and tension. To make matters worse, she is probably forced by the shortage of workers to carry the load which two foreign nurses should be sharing. This means long hours and scant rest. It is not surprising that a woman missionary of many years experience recently said, "I consider the work of the nurse the hardest job open to women on the foreign field."

Satisfactions. Yet the nurse's work is vital and satisfying. Her position is one rich in contacts and varied in opportunities for preaching Jesus Christ. It is with the touch of her hand that she preaches Him. Her sermons are her cheery smiles, her patient care, her gentle voice and ways; and the influence of her life she multiplies many times through the native nurses-in-training to whom she is an elder sister and whom she trains in technique and inspires in spirit.

Desirable Qualities. The qualifications of the foreign missionary which need emphasis in the case of the nurse are, in addition to good health, unfailing cheerfulness, good staying qualities, firmness and decision, capacity to direct and to impart, ability to carry out orders, and the knack of neatness and orderliness. For her preparation the nurse should add to a four-year high-school course, as a minimum, a three-year nurses' training course, and one year in a school of missions, or its equivalent, for a study of missions and the Bible. The work of training nurses, of superintending hospitals, of giving as well as taking detailed orders, and the growing specialization of medical missionary work increasingly call for thorough preparation for the nurse.

Statistics. Nurses are not listed separately in the missionary census. There are probably about five hundred in foreign missionary service. The call is for two hundred and five.

CHAPTER VIII
EDUCATIONAL MISSIONARY

When the missionary societies close their books and quit, leaving an independent national church in full possession of every field; and when "non-Christian" shall have become obsolete, no small part of the credit shall belong to the Christian teacher. It is true that the evangelist establishes and sustains, and that the physician opens fields and exemplifies the Christ life in healing; but it is also true that the teacher is indispensable for any complete Christianization of the world.

Indeed, fundamentally, the whole missionary enterprise is a matter of education. Preaching the gospel is an educational process. To convert a man means to bring him through a *knowledge* of God and into a personal *experience* which leads to changed *motives, attitudes,* and *behavior;* and all these are the familiar terms of educational psychology. Conversion itself, therefore, on the human side, is a schooling proposition. Schools took root and grew naturally in the soil of the mission compound.

Mission schools developed because they were needed to educate the Christian community and to train native helpers. They grew also because native schools, at the start almost wholly lacking, did not keep pace with the increasing readiness of the people for education. In the third place they grew because the missionary found his readiest approach to the people through the children, and because he found that the schools increased the permanence of his evangelistic efforts. From primary and village schools developed boarding and high schools, which overflowed into colleges and universities. The need for preacher, and, later, for teachers, Bible women, and physicians gave rise to the professional schools. Christian missions have carried the torch of modern education to the ends of the earth, but ignorance is not yet dispelled. To-day in India only one man in sixteen, only one Chinaman in twenty, one woman of India in one hundred, and one Chinese woman in three thousand[1] can read. Truly non-Christian lands are hardly promising territory for book agents!

Programme. The task before educational missions now, in addition to aiding in establishing adequate schools in countries where they do not exist and in helping to improve, through effective example, the systems already existing, is largely to mobilize missionary resources to educate the Christian youth of the Orient; to equip them with the economic, social, religious, and professional training necessary to assure self-respecting, independent churches and an aggressive Christian leadership for the East; to provide them with the knowledges and skills, the Christian faith and spirit, to go forth and help lead the world to the feet of the Good Teacher.

Brief mention of some of the broad problems which confront the Christian school in the East is essential to an understanding of the difficulties facing the individual teacher. In India, China, and Japan national systems

---

[1]Taylor, A. W., "Social Work of Christian Missions," Foreign Christian Missionary Society, Cincinnati, 1912, p. 163.

of education, which dominate these countries, are rapidly developing. Japan already has regulations which fall heavily upon all private schools. In Japan, the foreign teacher, even in mission schools, teaches only English and that only one or two hours a week to any one group.[1] Furthermore, even in mission schools, the amount of religious teaching is more or less regulated by government, compulsory teaching of religion being entirely prohibited.[2] In these Eastern countries the situation is rapidly becoming one where educational missions must accept a subordinate place. Competition with government schools, rapidly improving, amply financed, and largely attended, is out of the question.

Indeed, with the introduction of vocational, industrial, and agricultural training, the mission boards are hard pressed to maintain their position in the front rank. The new ideal of industrial education of the masses for economic efficiency, essential everywhere, but especially among Eastern Christians, calls for expensive equipment and increased outlay. The one clear principle which emerges at this stage from the puzzling consideration of such questions as the continued use of English in the classroom, of the employment of non-Christian teachers, of the pros and cons of accepting government aid, and of the forthcoming question of co-education is the imperative need for co-operative effort by denominational mission boards. Only by a pooling of resources can mission schools of higher education with requisite standards and adequate equipment be maintained. Already in China and Korea there are no less than fifty union undertakings of which twenty-five

---

[1]Report on Preparation of Educational Missionaries, Board of Missionary Preparation, 1916, p. 110.
[2]Op. Cit., p. 108.

are colleges and theological schools, and in which thirty-eight different missionary societies co-operate.[1]

Difficulties. In a field thus beset with problems it is not surprising that the foreign teacher himself faces difficulties of a large number, a very practical one being the lack of equipment. The erection and equipment of just one of a group of buildings of an American college of medium wealth cost more than all the buildings and equipment of Peking University.[2] Another is the lack of free time, a disadvantage felt by all conscientious, whole-hearted teachers everywhere, no doubt, but especially real to the missionary. The complete absorption of time and energy under the stress of daily duties and of continual contacts with students in class, on campus, and in home quarters, not to be avoided but rather sought for the work's sake, drains nervous energy and leaves no time for private study or coveted research.

Then there is the problem of mastering the vernacular when the educational missionary teaches in schools where, as in India or Japan, the class-work, or his part in the class-work, calls for English. The students are apt to encourage his use of the English and natural inclination may pull that way, too, but as a missionary his success in touching lives and transforming character awaits a thorough knowledge of the native tongue. Without that he cannot hope to enter the lives of the people nor can he hope to interpret their point of view. To understand the native point of view is perhaps the hardest problem of the foreign Christian teacher. He must not only put his words into their language but he

[1]Dennett, Tyler, "Missionary Schoolmaster," Joint Centenary Commission, Methodist Episcopal, 111 Fifth Avenue, New York City, p. 22.
[2]Report on Preparation of Educational Missionaries, Board of Missionary Preparation, New York City, 1916, p. 81.

must put his ideas into their thoughts. He must regard racial as well as individual differences, the problem varying with types and conditions. There is the meditative Indian, the practical Chinaman, the suspicious Turk, the poetical Latin, and there is the complex situation where conditions are heterogeneous and unsystematic, as in a case at Anatolia College in Turkey where, of 120 students entering at one time, 113 were irregular, having studied in Turkish, Armenian, Greek, Russian, French, and Protestant schools;[1] but in every field this task of understanding the pupil and beginning with him where he is taxes the teacher to the uttermost. Unless he somehow get inside the native and see out through his eyes, and pulsate with his heartbeats, the missionary teacher fails.

Satisfactions. The teacher's compensations are not to be overlooked, however. In some respects, especially in comparison with the general evangelistic missionary, whose constituency shifts and who must itinerate much, the teacher works in connection with a comparatively permanent community, a community where he enjoys the bracing and congenial comradeship of faculty and students. In addition to the fact that the schools themselves are popular, the teacher enjoys throughout the Orient to a degree unknown in the West a respect and esteem which greatly enhances his more or less extended influence with his students. Mission schools are largely responsible for the awakening of the East. Their graduates have become leaders of note and power. One mission school in Shanghai trained three of the leading Chinese diplomats of recent years. In India

---

[1] Op. Cit., p. 101.

the government is turning to the graduates of mission schools for leaders. To touch the lives of the most virile and high-charactered youth of the awakening East, at the time of greatest susceptibility, "while the clay is on the wheel," and in the relationship of greatest influence, that of teacher, is indeed an opportunity beyond price, resulting in this fine reward: that "in living letters" his message goes forth to help remake the world.

Desirable Qualities. The rewards of the teacher depend upon the teacher's spirit. He must above all else have the missionary motive. To missionary patriotism, which means an irresistible passion to convert the world, every other quality must be subordinate in those who enlist for service in the missionary "expeditionary force." This point needs emphasis because the teacher is inclined to enjoy a sense of self-sufficiency with teaching in itself, especially in this age which exalts socialized education as the panacea for all ills. For the person who goes merely to teach there is no room on the missionary transport, because native schools and teachers are already on the field and growing more effective every day. The educational missionary must be more than a teacher. In the words of Barton, he is to be every inch and every moment a missionary.

In addition to patience, adaptability, sense of humor, refinement, courtesy, self-control, and capacity for teamwork, which may be called seven invariables for all missionaries, the teacher should possess breadth of vision, keen insight, loyalty to truth, an appreciative attitude, seeing and appropriating the good wherever found, well-developed imaginative power, and a "sensible stubbornness," which will prevent his skidding at once into the old ruts at the first encounter with conservative leadership on the field. To count for most his must be a pervasive personality, that sum total of an attractive, sociable, tactful, sympathetic, strong individuality. Of course, above all else he must be able to teach. He needs to be a good "conductor of ideas."

Preparation. The preparation of the educational missionary depends somewhat upon the country to which he is to go and the position he is to fill. In details it therefore varies widely, but in main outlines his studies can be suggested. He cannot hope to be found acceptable with less than a college course of four years and at least one year of specialized educational study. His general college course should include the following subjects[1]:

English literature.
At least one modern language.
A science with emphasis on scientific method.
History.
Sociology and economics.
Biblical history and literature.
English composition and public speaking.
Psychology.
Philosophy.
Fundamental Christian principles.

Among the professional subjects which are suggested for his year or more of specialization are the following[2]:

The philosophy of education.
Educational psychology.
Educational sociology.

[1] Op. Cit., p. 216.
[2] Op. Cit., 217.

The principles of teaching.

Teaching methods.

Comparative educational methods.

History of education with emphasis on supervision, observation, and practice teaching.

The principles and methods of religious education.

During his period of graduate study the candidate should review his Biblical studies, and take advantage of every opportunity to inspect educational plants, studying their methods, equipment, and curricula. The movement is growing to consider the first term on the field and the first furlough as a part of the period of preparation. This will mean supervision of the five or seven years in service and the extension of the first furlough to include a year of graduate study leading, perhaps, to the A.M. or Ph. D. degree.

Up to the present time the educational missionaries who have gone out for specific teaching positions have been comparatively few. Perhaps four-fifths of those occupying teaching positions have been general ordained missionaries, called after two to five years' experience in evangelistic work[1]. Many missionaries preach and teach at the same time. This condition is rapidly changing. At the present time, while the majority of all the teachers in mission schools are native, the tendency toward specialization is creating a demand for educational specialists. What has been said about the work, the problems and compensations, the qualifications and preparation, of the educational missionary will in general apply to each of the following types of worker: boarding and high-school teachers and principals, college and

---

[1]Estimate of Dr. S. J. Corey, op. cit., p. 209.

university instructors, professors in professional schools, industrial-school teachers, school superintendents, matrons, elementary-school teachers and supervisors and kindergartners.

Statistics. The total educational calls are, men, 290; women, 365. The study of one thousand ex-missionaries indicated that fifty-four per cent of educational missionaries served five years or less, due partly no doubt to short terms.

CHAPTER IX

OTHER MISSIONARY SPECIALISTS

The call for teachers described in the last chapter indicates the extent to which the era of specialization has reached the mission field. Boards are faced with the necessity of providing workers who have attained proficiency in other lines than theology and medicine. This need varies with countries and with localities. Fields ready for one type of specialization may not yet demand others. Especially, however, where large groups of missionaries are associated economy of effort and efficiency of result more and more require that certain men be set apart for specialized work.

This demand gains ground not without the opposition of some who, believing that it is not special training but native ability that counts, labor under the impression that a specialist is one of narrow training whose expertness in one line will not make up for his ignorance and insufficiency in the broader equipment of large vision, many-sided interests, and ready adaptability which the world-wide enterprise of missions must always require of its recruits. The mission boards realize the importance of natural capacity and of broad education as a basis for specialization, and are careful to see to it that on the mission field the specialist shall always be a "broad man sharpened to a point."

From replies received from 143 missionaries on the field to questions as to the present lack of workers with specialized training and as to what kinds of special training are most needed, the Board of Missionary Preparation recently prepared a list containing fifty types of workers. In addition, teachers for ten different subjects were mentioned.[1] Industrial workers, teachers of science, Sunday-school specialists, general social-service workers, association secretaries, and business managers were mentioned most frequently. Some of the more unusual needs, appearing at least once in the list, were for a university-extension worker, a dentist, an optician, an alienist, a music-teacher, a city evangelistic worker, a specialist in phonetics, a sanitation expert, an institutional church worker, a Boy Scout worker, a statistician, a specialist in international law, and a journalist. To meet the needs which this study reveals will require that mission stations inform their boards of their needs long enough in advance to allow the boards time to select candidates and to make definite assignments long enough ahead to permit the specialized training required. It further suggests the need of going more thoroughly into the special fitness of volunteers, together with the adoption of a policy of turning over to other boards with vacancies those with special qualifications for whom no place exists.

Difficulties and Satisfactions. The problems which confront the specialist on the field are those of all missionaries, with one or two of his very own. To begin with, he may not always find awaiting him the exact job for which he has prepared. All missionary workers are more or less subject to emergency calls and shifts in position. These, while growing less frequent, are

---

[1] "Specialized Training of Missionaries," Board of Missionary Preparation, New York, 1920, pp. 15-18.

never to be wholly done away with; and they will always hit hardest the specialist. Then, too, the work which he undertakes, by the very nature of the case, is apt to be in an undeveloped state, affording many disappointments in the slow progress of his ambitious plans. He will also as a specialist be cut off from participation in the broader evangelistic work and from stimulating contact with it. Compensation for him, on the other hand, consists in concentrating and not scattering his effort, in doing a specific task well, and in feeling himself an effective part in the great missionary machine. If he have the spirit of the pioneer, he thrills in the unrestricted opportunities in his field for initiating new projects significant for missions and for the world.

Desirable Qualities. As in the case of the teacher, without the missionary spirit, regardless of his intellectual endowments, the specialist does more harm than good. He must be in Asia primarily for the glory of God. It is peculiarly important, also, that he have the ability to get along well with other people, because his work tends to set him apart, making friction and misunderstanding likely where there ought to be co-operation and mutual helpfulness; for the specialist is in a very true sense the servant of the whole missionary community. Executive ability, the capacity to set others to work, is for him invaluable. Above all, he must be a practical man who can make the most of adverse circumstances. If he is a specialist, "strong in theory and weak in practice, effective only in the most favorable surroundings,'" he will surely fail.

---

[1] "Specialized Training of Missionaries," p. 63.

Preparation. As indicated in the last chapter, the minimum general education for the specialist, except in certain cases of skilled helpers, should be four years, followed by a period varying in length for special preparation, supervised by the mission board. The utilization of the first term and of the first furlough for further study is becoming increasingly desirable. What has been said so far applies in large measure to all specialists. It remains in concluding this survey of foreign-missionary workers to describe briefly the background and the work of several of the increasingly significant types of specialist.

I. THE AGRICULTURIST

Christian evangelists, physicians, and teachers have preached, healed, and taught, to save the Orient; and now to save the Orient Christian agriculturists are ploughing. In these days, when it is realized that the economics of a people must be taken into account as well as its health and its intellect, the redemption of the world presents a four-sided challenge, spiritual, social, intellectual, and economic; and the importance of the last, especially in the backward, sub-productive non-Christian lands is just now claiming much attention. If the first task of missions is to make Christians, the second is to make self-respecting and self-supporting Christians. In the Orient, which is perhaps seventy-five per cent rural, where famine and want stalk in the wake of the methods of forty centuries, and where the church enrolls the poorest rather than the well-to-do, this means the teaching and demonstrating of modern agriculture. As missionary strategy this appears to be, in the words of Mott, "coming at the heart of the people by the most direct approach."[1]

Programme. The programme of the agriculturist centres in a demonstration farm where modern methods and modern equipment are put to work in the interest of bigger, better crops and finer stock. This farm becomes the laboratory of an agricultural college to train farm specialists who go out as teachers and apostles of prosperity. At this centre are offered short courses for the farmers of the community, who come for a few weeks during slack seasons. From these centres workers go out to conduct farmers' institutes and demonstrations, and to distribute seeds. Courses are also offered for native teachers from village schools, who carry back the message of increased productivity and plenty. Not the least effect of the agricultural movement in the East, especially in India, is the new dignity of labor, which it preaches alike to high caste and low.

All India has come to peer wide-eyed over the fence into the magic 275-acre farm of Sam Higginbottom at Allahabad, where, with a dormitory providing for 100 students, and with sixty head of high-grade cattle, fifty oxen, seven silos, American machinery, and a great well for irrigation supplying a million gallons a day, he is demonstrating how "English seed planted in Indian soil by American methods" can increase the native yield of wheat from six to fifty-six bushels an acre. Thus does this new missionary specialist "interpret the Christian message in terms of agricultural welfare." The boards are calling for forty agriculturists now.

---

[1]From a letter to the International Association of Agricultural Missions, in session in New York City, December 7, 1920.

II. The Social Engineer

The East needs technical engineers to survey continents, construct steel highways, span great rivers, and to modernize the life of half the world; but the East needs most of all Christian social engineers to construct through the heart of dense populations clean highways to God, to bridge the gulf of caste, and to Christianize the social life of races which are just now falling prey to the evils of an industrial age, evils which in overtaking them add to the great moral havoc of non-Christian lands. In Japan from 1883 to 1916 the number of factories increased from 125 with 15,000 operatives to 20,000 with a million operatives. In these factories in 1914 there were 471,000 women and children, twenty-two per cent of the children being under fourteen.[1]

Programme. The work of the Christian social worker consists in making social surveys; in establishing settlements, which shall spread their roots into the life of communities through genuine, helpful service; and in training native social workers. The policy at present advocated is the establishment of a few strong centres, operated from the first with native partnership, and to make these demonstration and training centres. The best preparation for this worker, after a college course and a year of special social-religious education, is an apprenticeship in the slums at home, for the task in the foreign field is similar to the task at home, with greater need and greater opportunity. The foreign-missionary task, while not less a project of individual soul-saving,

---

[1]Lambuth, Walter R., "Medical Missions," Student Volunteer Movement, New York, 1920, p. 167.

becomes more and more a complex undertaking for saving the soul of society. Not fewer than twenty-five women and seven men are being called for social service.

III. THE MISSIONARY WRITER

Although illiteracy is still high in non-Christian lands, the work of the schools is constantly increasing the size of the reading public. The native church-membership in the East, numbering upwards of six hundred thousand, and the upper classes in all the countries present a large and growing market for books and magazines. Books of apologetics, commentaries, sermons, books on the life of Christ, biographies, devotional books, works on reform, fiction with a Christian flavor, Sunday-school literature, and text-books are all needed in the mission field, not to mention periodicals, theological journals, and magazines and papers for women and children. In the press of missionary activities this field has developed out of all proportion to the means for meeting it; and anti-Christian literature flourishes amazingly. Growing literacy, the awakening of religious and social consciousness, and the whetting of intellect, which missions themselves have done so much to hasten, create a challenge for literary work of large magnitude, and make the writer and editor an indispensable agent of the missionary enterprise.

The work, embodying supervision of printing, publishing, office-management, editorial supervision, proof-reading, examination of manuscripts, translation, and authorship, is open only to an experienced missionary, who is set apart for a limited period only, returning later to other fields of activity. Such a man is chosen because he possesses a readiness to appreciate and appropriate the good in other systems and in other people, because he understands the history, the life, and the needs of the people about him; because he exhibits no unkind spirit of attack in dealing with other religions and literatures; because of his high scholarship and linguistic ability; and, finally, because of his capacity to write, for above all he must have "ink in the blood."

Since no missionary recruit finds a literary position immediately waiting for him on the field, and probably no one ever will, a special preparation before going to the field is out of the question. However, while making the preparation for whatever other position he is to fill, the recruit who craves the opportunity in time of speaking the words of life through the printed page might well seek experience in a printing or publishing establishment in the home land, in writing for newspapers, in journalism and authorship.

IV. The Business Manager

An enterprise which has a pay-roll of eleven thousand foreign missionaries and a budget of thirty million dollars may well have need of capable business men who specialize in the business end of the enterprise. In addition to the college and university business managers there is the mission treasurer and the business agent. The mission treasurer is the distributing agent for the funds from America. As a specialist in foreign exchange and finance he becomes an invaluable adviser to missionaries; and to the efficiency and success of the business of missions his accuracy and his systematic methods are vital.

The business agent, almost as essential, living usually at a seaport city, is the man who does what no one

else has time to do. He is the janitor of foreign missions, keeping things generally in order. His work is
varied and often annoying, calling for a large fund of
miscellaneous knowledge, constant alertness, and business gumption. He does everything from reading time-
tables, employing coolies, and dealing with government
agents to ordering goods from Sears, Roebuck, and Company, and shopping for a missionary's family. He is
one of the men W. C. Willoughby must have had in
mind when he wrote, "If you are able to sweep a floor
to the glory of God, why, you are the man we want; and
we want you badly." There are opportunities now for
twenty business agents and treasurers.

V. SKILLED HELPERS

The present needs of the foreign-missionary organization afford also opportunities for the architect, the
builder, the printer, the bookkeeper, and the steno-
grapher. Until now these positions have been filled
largely by the part-time employment of regular missionaries. The work, the routine, the difficulties, the satisfactions, and the qualifications belonging to these types
of service need no description. To the extent that the
specialty predominates in each case there will be parallel-
ism with similar positions at home; to the extent that the
missionary element predominates, the worker will share
the joys and sorrows of other missionaries. The preparation of this group of specialists, with the possible
exception of the architect, calls for a minimum general
education of high-school grade, while the one prerequisite
for every person sent out by any board at any time to
any field for any work is a Christian faith and a missionary spirit. Within the group of occupation here

described are openings now for about twenty women and thirty-five men.

In considering the extent to which this division of labor promises to go on the mission field, as well as in recalling the varied types of workers already enlisted in evangelism, medicine, education, and social service, one realizes that against a world need Christian missions offers a world programme.

The outstanding problem of this world programme, affecting more or less every foreign worker everywhere, is the need for him to decrease while the native church increases. This condition which must be more and more faced by Western Christian workers in the East is splendidly illustrated by an incident in the case of Japan. It has to do with the buying of Western street-cars. Bishop Tucker[1] tells how at first the Japanese, carried away with enthusiasm for everything Western, purchased electric tramways of the same dimensions as those used in America. These were very comfortable for the American missionaries, but the seats did not fit the short Japanese. This continued for a time, but now it is noticeable that the Western street-cars in Japan have lower, narrower seats. While they are less comfortable for the foreigner, they fit the Japanese exactly. Thus the Oriental is learning to adapt Western ideas.

Another observation which may well be made before bringing this part to a close is to suggest that the vestibule to foreign-missionary work is a man's own church and community at home. These pages have set forth a high standard, both as to personality and preparation, a standard which, while far more flexible than here ap-

---

[1] Report of Conference on Preparation of Educational Missionaries, Board of Missionary Preparation, p. 112.

pears, should be more and more maintained.   However, fundamentally the one indispensable characteristic for foreign service is a missionary spirit, and the one indispensable preparation is an apprenticeship which enables one to win souls.   That is why candidate secretaries and experienced missionaries suggest that the best time and place to test one's native qualifications and to begin preparing is here and now.   One can write his mission board, becoming acquainted with its departments and secretaries.   He can begin reading the lives of the great heroes of missions.   He can study the maps of the Orient.   He can teach a Sunday-school class, lead an Endeavor society, lead in mission-study, volunteer foi Y. M. C. A. committee work, or undertake to help in a social settlement.   Unless one can grip twelve-year-olds here how can he hope to grip them over there?   Unless one can testify effectively in English here how can he hope to testify effectively in Chinese over there?   When Miss Amanda Jefferson, thirty years a missionary in Ratnagiri, India, was talking about her work, she said with a significant smile, ''You know, I got my training for calling in the zenanas of India from my settlement work in New York City.''

Finally, one is impressed in studying the varied phases of the missionary programme by finding how similar is the task overseas to the task at home.   This is especially true in the newer fields of educational specialization, agriculture, and social service, although it is also increasingly present in the work of the foreign minister and physician as well.   After such a study one can sympathize with the growing tendency to erase the words ''foreign'' and ''home,'' to write in their place, ''world-wide.''   Yet one realizes that from the point of view of the worker the ocean still pushes in between home base and mission field, and that the foreign missionary is foreign missionary still, as of old the most highly selected Christian worker, as well he may be, for he serves "the most powerful international and inter-racial constructive force that the world has ever known."[1]

[1]Fisher, Galen M., "My Place in the World's Work," Student Volunteer Movement, p. 17.

REFERENCES

PART II

GENERAL

a. Moore, E. C., "Expansion of Christianity in the Modern World," University of Chicago Press, 1919.

b. Walsh, W. P., "Modern Heroes of the Mission Field," Fleming H. Revell Company, New York.

c. Speer, R. E., "What Constitutes a Missionary Call?" Student Volunteer Movement, New York.

d. World Reconstruction Papers, Series 2, Student Volunteer Movement, New York.

e. "Call, Qualifications, Preparation, of Missionary Candidates," Student Volunteer Movement, New York, 1906.

f. Murray, J., Lovell, "World Friendship, Inc.," Missionary Education Movement, New York, 1921.

g. Harrington, C. K., "Captain Bickel of the Inland Seas," Fleming H. Revell Company, New York.

h. Waldo, Fullerton L., "With Grenfell on the Labrador," Fleming H. Revell Company, New York, 1920.

i. "Survey of the Effect of War upon Missions" (series), *International Review of Missions*, October, 1919, pp. 433-90.

j. Baird, Annie, "Inside Views of Mission Life," Westminster Press, Philadelphia, 1913.

k. Six pamphlets on preparation for special fields, (1) China, (2) India, (3) Japan, (4) Latin America, (5) Near East, (6) Pagan Africa, Board of Missionary Preparation, New York.

l. Three pamphlets on the presentation of Christianity in (1) Confucian lands, (2) to Hindoos, and (3) to Moslems, Board of Missionary Preparation, New York.

CHAPTER VI

m. Brown, A. J., "Rising Churches in Non-Christian Lands," Methodist Book Concern, 1915.

n. Carvell, A. M., "In Jungle Depths," London Religious Tract Society, 1919.

o. "Report of the Conference on Preparation of Ordained Missionaries," held in New York, Dec. 1, 2, 1914, Board of Missionary Preparation, New York.

p. "Preparation of Women for Foreign-Missionary Service," Board of Missionary Preparation, New York.

q. Platt, Mary S., "Home with the Open Door," Student Volunteer Movement, New York, 1920.

CHAPTER VII

r. Lambuth, Walter R., "Medical Missions," Student Volunteer Movement, New York, 1920.

s. Franklin, James H., "Ministers of Mercy," Missionary Education Movement, New York, 1919.

t. "Qualifications and Preparation of Medical Missionaries and Nurses," Board of Missionary Preparation, New York.

u. Weaver, E. W., "Medicine as a Profession," Chapter XX, A. S. Barnes, New York, 1917.

CHAPTER VIII

v. Barton, James L., "Educational Missions," Student Volunteer Movement, New York, 1917.

w. "Report of the Conference on Preparation of Educational Missionaries," held in New York, Dec. 4, 5, 1916, Board of Missionary Preparation, New York.

CHAPTER IX

x. Clough, John E., "Social Christianity in the Orient," Macmillan, New York.

y. "Specialized Training of Missionaries," Board of Missionary Preparation, New York.

z "Preparation of Missionaries for Literary Work," Board of Missionary Preparation, New York.

ASSIGNMENTS

PART II

CHAPTER VI

* What foreign missionary do you know or have you heard? What has impressed you most about him (or her)?

* The work of the general missionary is said to be the most comprehensive type of religious work. Why?

1. Estimate the total annual income of a missionary family at the time it has been twenty years in service and the four children are respectively five, eight, twelve, and sixteen, the eldest having returned to the United States to live with an aunt and attend college.

2. Use Paul to illustrate the work of the foreign missionary, applying the paragraph headings of this chapter as an outline for a study of his life.

3. How does missionary preparation for India differ from that for China? (See k.)

CHAPTER VII

4. Give illustrations from biography of the peculiar difficulties and satisfactions of the medical missionary. (See s.)

CHAPTER VIII

5. What reasons can you give for the use of English in higher education in the Orient? (See v.)

6. What are hostels, and the work of those in charge of them? (See f, chapter, ''Gateways to the Mind.'')

7. Outline in brief the vocational steps in the life of at least one notable missionary educator. (See f.)

CHAPTER IX

* What type of specialized missionary work do you consider most permanent and promising?

8. Outline the arguments raised against specialization, and refute them.
9. Would you say that it is part of the missionary's work to improve social conditions of a country? If so, how can he best achieve this end? (See f, chapter on social conditions.)

In General

* What do you consider woman's most important work in the foreign missionary enterprise?

10. Group the desirable qualifications for a foreign missionary under three heads such as essential, desirable, accessory. (See d, number 12.)
11. Who should not go as missionaries? (See e.)
12. Describe some unique missionary vocations. (See h.)
13. Interview a foreign missionary, seeking in your report to modify or amplify the information already available.
14. Study and be prepared to advise the subject of case 1, of case 3, of case 6, of case 9.
15. Select the chief difficulty and the chief desirable quality which are most nearly distinctive of each type of worker considered.
16. For a special project for Part II, see Appendix 3.

PART III

THE DEACONESS AND LAY WORKER

"'He carved his own way to his place of influence. You might put such a man anywhere, and his natural qualities would assert themselves. Patiently, industriously, lovingly, he toiled for others. With splendid self-forgetfulness and with passionate devotion to his risen Lord he wrought and gave his life. 'He that loseth his own life shall find it unto life eternal.' '"*

*George A. Warburton's tribute to Robert R. McBurney, a layman whose qualities may well be emulated by all religious workers.

137

"For even as we have many members in one body, and all the members have not the same office: so we who are many, are one body in Christ * * * and having gifts differing according to the grace that was given us * * *"

I will do my best, with what I have, where I am, for Jesus Christ to-day.

CHAPTER X

THE ASSOCIATION SECRETARY

I. The Y. W. C. A.

Less than a century ago woman's place was home; to-day she is at home everywhere. This has come about gradually. At first her outside activities were counted on the fingers of one hand. An early record of the Young Women's Christian Association, established in Boston in' 1866, enumerates sixteen callings followed by its members. To-day in commerce, industry, and even the professions, women work in hundreds of vocations. The first co-educational college class was graduated at Oberlin in 1841. Now thousands of women enroll in colleges, universities, professional schools, and in music and art schools in the larger centres. Steadily woman has taken line after line of defence; and schools, offices, factories, cities, have fallen before the young woman's march upon the world.

Mary Antin's wistful voyage overseas from Russia to the "promised land," typical of many an immigrant's experiences, is symbolic also of many hundreds and thousands of American girls who have made a no less fateful pilgrimage, no less fraught with hardships and heartaches, from the open country and the village and the town to the promised city.

Programme. This situation gave birth to the Young Women's Christian Association, which, historically speaking, entered the world very humbly through a boarding-house door. It emerged first in the busy, crowded city to meet the needs of homeless, self-supporting girls. This need it met with a home which was first of all Christian, for from the beginning until now its corner-stone has been "soul-winning and Christian character-building." But it soon became more than a home. While continuing to hold stanchly to the requirement that its voting membership must belong to evangelical churches, it early developed, in the face of a great need and a great response, a wide-open door to womanhood everywhere. Its programme to-day includes the promotion of physical, social, mental, and spiritual growth through gymnasium, club, classes in academic, vocational, and practical arts, through Bible-study, devotional meetings, and practical Christian service. It *came* to minister to the needs of the girls away from home, but because it stands for exalting the individual girl as a girl, for affording wholesome social intercourse, for "tending human needs in a helpful human way," the Y. W. C. A. has *remained* to minister to all the needs of all the women of the whole community, and to become a strong, world-wide social force for the extension of the democracy of God.

The general Association work is organized on the basis of city, county, student, and town units, above these being the regional and national administrative and departmental offices. The Student Associations in the colleges and universities, in close co-operation with the Student Y. M. C. A. and the Student Volunteer Movement, carry on the general programme, modified to meet student conditions. In addition to the religious, social, physical, and mental, the phases of activity include employment, lodgment, travellers' aid, girls' industrial, and social-service departments. In addition to national executives and field-secretaries, full-time departmental specialists in increasing numbers carry on this varied enterprise. However, the general secretaryship of the normal city Association may be considered at the present time as the dominant Y. W. C. A. vocation.

Routine. The "city general" leads a varied life. She attends and perhaps leads the daily staff devotional meeting. This staff consists of five to eight or more workers, according to the size of the Association, which for a city of a hundred and fifty thousand population has perhaps 2,500 members. During the morning she may confer with one or two members of her staff individually. Probably she calls by appointment upon an influential member of the board. Every day or two she attends a committee meeting within the Association, and two or three times a week she may attend a committee meeting of outside agencies. Every week she presides at the regular staff meeting. Never a month passes without an invitation to address some civic, religious, or other organization. With personal and group conferences, with meetings inside and outside the organization, her mornings, afternoons, and evenings will slip by, for she feels that she must in addition be in evidence at every evening programme of the Association.

Yet her work cannot be scheduled by the clock or by the day. Indeed, it is not the actual tasks which she shoulders that are really significant. The actual detail she shifts as much as possible, holding part of her work to consist in being always free for emergencies, in order to be where most needed when needed most. Her big perpetual job is to permeate every inch of the premises and every heart of the membership with genuine friendliness, with democratic sociability, and with a real Christian spirit which seeks daily opportunity for personal religious service; for she is both a community hostess and a Christian evangelist.

Difficulties. The hardest problems which the general secretary faces grow out of the double basis of membership, which provides that, while all are to be admitted without restriction to associate membership, only members of those churches eligible to participation in the Federal Council of Churches may vote or hold office. In meeting its responsibility to the community, the Y. W. C. A. admits an increasing number of girls who are not eligible to voting membership.

The general secretary bears the brunt of this embarrassing situation in at least three ways. In exemplifying and emphasizing the Christian life and character, which she must do in loyalty to the traditions and purposes of the Association, she is misunderstood, considered narrow, and shunned by the girls whom she most wishes to reach. When she goes into the community, she finds a feeling of dissatisfaction on the ground that the Y. W. C. A. is undemocratic in denying a voice in its government to so many who belong to it and support it. On the other hand, when she goes out in a campaign for funds among the influential Christian supporters, she faces another criticism that the Y. W. C. A. has ceased to be a Christian institution because it serves those of other creeds and races!

Obstacles of a more personal nature confront the

secretary as well. To keep herself wholly human, sympathetic, and approachable is not easy. To be dependent upon a volunteer leadership which can be built up only with great difficulty because of shifting membership is another trial. To prevent the growth of clique and class where freedom and preference in grouping is encouraged is not easy. Finally, the general secretary gives up to her work many opportunities for outside social life, for concerts, for the society of men friends, which other young women enjoy, not to be passed over too lightly. Heading a Y. W. C. A. is not a vacation undertaking or a season's adventure. It is one of the exacting, purposeful life-work callings, demanding for success conviction, courage, and consecration.

Satisfactions. ''That they might have life and that they might have it more abundantly,'' is the ambition of the Y. W. C. A. secretary for her girls. And they do. Under her eyes every day she sees them living the life more abundant. This is her compensation. The splendid response of the young womanhood of America to the open door of the Y. W. C. A. gives the secretary the opportunity to reach scores and hundreds of girls at the point of their greatest need. She has the joy of bringing together girls of different interests and attainments for their mutual advantage and for the gain of the social, economic, and spiritual democracy of to-morrow.

As her Association builds itself into the life of the people and the institutions about it, and as she becomes a respected and recognized leader of the womanhood of the community, she enjoys the privilege of helping employers and employees understand each

other, of influencing far-reaching betterment mea
ures, and of co-operating effectively with the churche
The secretaryship affords also through the facing o
many needs, the initiating of large plans, and throug'
many stimulating contacts great opportunity for personal growth, thus again proving that compensations
are commensurate with difficulties.

Desirable Qualities. "Idealism tempered with common sense" is a very desirable qualification in the
general secretary, as are also a delightful sense of humor and a practical sense of proportion.

This last is necessary to keep her from getting tan-
gled in red tape or lost in odds and ends of routine.
She must possess the ability to organize and train
workers about a work rather than followers about a
leader. She who can design and construct an Association programme and then slip out of the scheme
without a collapse of the enterprise is the one needed
in the Y. W. C. A. secretaryship. She must know how
to make herself scaffolding and not keystone to the
work. Serenity, of that kind which can face responsibility, threatened confusion, unexpected obstacles, and
multiplying annoyances without a panic, but with effective calm and with confidence—inspiring poise, is
of paramount importance for the successful secretary.
Such a serene disposition finds its source in part from
inherited sound nerves, in part from acquired habit
of action, and in large part from constant and abundant spiritual anointing at the foot of the cross. The
Y. W. C. A. secretaryship is a woman-size job which
calls for unusual qualities of leadership and adaptability.

Preparation. A college course or its equivalent and a professional Association training of one year in the national training-school or its equivalent are essential for the Y. W. C. A. secretary. Business experience as an employed person, working with other people in a capacity of leadership, is also regarded as a splendid asset. An equivalent to a college education would be a normal-school course supplemented by summer work at a university. An equivalent to the year in the training-school would be actual successful work in Y. W. C. A. leadership, rounded out with extension courses and supervised apprenticeship. The courses given in the training-school in New York City include technical courses in the history, principles, and methods of Association work, classes in the Bible, comparative religions, sociology, and kindred subjects. The prominent position of the secretary in the community and the breadth of the national Y. W. C. A. programme, the growth of half a century of successful experience, demand trained leadership.

Foreign Secretaryship. Overseas Association work is firmly planted, the scope of the movement being the same there as here. The policy always is to make the organization indigenous. Native volunteer leadership is developed. Self-support is encouraged. The foreign secretary is, therefore, one who must have large capacity for adaptation, for allowing herself to be used for the carrying out of the plans of those among whom she works. There are calls for eighty overseas Y. W. C. A. secretaries.

Statistics. The twelve hundred Associations and approximately five hundred fifty thousand members of the

Y. W. C. A. employ no fewer than four thousand secretaries, including a national staff of about four hundred. The "city general" in a city of one hundred to two hundred thousand is paid between $1,800 and $2,500 a year. The Y. W. C. A. has openings for eight hundred to a thousand secretaries every year.

II. THE Y. M. C. A.

"I beg your pardon, can you direct me to the Y. M. C. A.?" strangers in town frequently ask; how frequently, would be worth knowing. Some present-day institutions people take for granted. The telephone is one; the post-office is one; another is the Young Men's Christian Association, which fits in so naturally and fills so useful and permanent a place in the community that one cannot imagine a city getting on without it. Yet this organization had its beginning less than eighty years ago in a little back room of a dry-goods house in London, its purpose meekly stated, "to improve the spiritual condition of young men engaged in the drapery and other trades."

That first Y. M. C. A. was a fire kindled in the heart of a prairie. It spread because the world was waiting for it and because it made a successful appeal to the young man universal. This *"high-class, far-sighted investment in the greatest undeveloped resources in the world—young men"* has had an open and a wide field, which it yet only begins to occupy. There are in the United States alone to-day, between the ages of fifteen and twenty-nine, no fewer than fifteen million young men, every one of whom is a Y. M. C. A. prospect.

Programme. To understand the spirit and purpose

of the Y. M. C. A., one must turn back to its beginnings, there to learn that it was prepared for by a young man's zeal and success in personal soul-saving, that it found its earliest activity in prayer meetings and Bible-study, and that its first and permanent statement of principle declared that it "seeks to unite those young men who, regarding Jesus Christ as their God and Saviour, according to the Holy Scriptures, desire to be His disciples in their doctrine and in their life, and to associate their efforts for the extension of His kingdom among young men.'"[1] Aggressive religious work and helping men to know and serve Jesus are the supreme mission from which the Association has never departed. The last request of Robert R. McBurney, thirty-six years general secretary of the New York City Y. M. C. A., whose life and work personify the secretaryship, was that the only talks at his funeral might be to urge young men to personal work for leading men to Christ. The comprehensive, many-sided programme which in its endeavor to translate Christianity in terms of the whole man the Association has built up about the familiar triangle of body, mind, and spirit is but the necessary expansion when a prayer meeting attempts to put its arms around the young manhood of the world.

Routine. A war poster described the Y. M. C. A. secretary as a well-rounded man, able to do a little of everything. This characterization evidently still applies, because a list of 150 possible duties attributed to him by Paul Super[2] includes such items as lending

---

[1] "The Paris Declaration," 1855, still the basis for active membership.

[2] Super, Paul, "Training a Staff," Association Press, New York, 1920, an excellent book.

money, teaching games, operating soda-fountains, assigning lockers, running movies, leading singing, hiring help, writing advertisements, balancing the cash, keeping abreast of the times, and learning people's names. However, when one realizes that the secretary may serve an Association having from one thousand to eight thousand members, with a staff of from six to thirty, more than four hundred Associations now employing a staff of four or more, one knows that the general secretary of the Y. M. C. A. is something more than a Jack of all trades. In order to conserve time and energy, he discriminates in values; he organizes men, measures, and methods; he assigns and supervises work to develop his staff; he manages men, presides at meetings, inspires and shepherds his membership. His is an all-round job, predominantly executive in nature.

Consider the general secretary of a city Association of about three thousand members, with a staff of perhaps fourteen. His day begins with the staff devotional meeting at nine. Correspondence and dictation come next, with several interruptions from members of the staff who come for individual help or advice. By noon he has made a tour of inspection of the building, accepted an invitation to speak in the near future at some gathering, has promised to attend a church-board meeting, which as a good churchman he cannot overlook; has made an engagement for luncheon with a business man whom he is attempting to interest in the work of the Y. M. C. A., and has had half a dozen interviews, ranging from one with a boy who comes with a letter of introduction asking his help to get a job, with whom he takes this opportunity of making a warm personal contact, to dealing with an irate youth who has lost something in the dormitory and threatens to sue the Association, and whose unfortunate experience of losing money or overcoat the secretary finds a way of turning to such unexpected account as to make a warm personal friend or a confessed follower of Christ.

When the executive gets back to the office from his engagement, he finds time for a confidential, heart-to-heart talk with a member of his staff who is discouraged and failing in his work. Perhaps it is the day of the staff meeting, in which case he goes in to this prepared to attend closely to reports, amending, criticising, and commending; to suggest and encourage new plans; to weld into one united programme each man's separate undertaking; and to send the men back to their tasks with fresh enthusiasm and deepened spiritual power. If this meeting ends in time, he perhaps gets into the gymnasium to finish off the day with volley-ball and a plunge, seeking the opportunity at once to mix with the men and to keep himself fit. The chances are more than even that he is kept at the office for the evening with committee meetings or other group gatherings. He has a long, full day into which, holding back a reserve for any emergency, he puts much of brain and heart and personality.

Difficulties. The matter of long hours is one of the problems of the Y. M. C. A. secretary. This "hard, every-day drudgery of persistent, constant living and working with men for men" requires more provision than it usually gets for the rest and the spiritual, mental, and physical replenishing without which a man cannot keep at his best. Another constant source of anxiety is the staff meeting. To get men there on time, to avoid monotony and keep out of a rut, to hold discussion centred on main issues, to prevent the necessarily business-like tone of the meeting from crowding out altogether the note of inspiration; in short, to make this weekly or bi-weekly gathering what it ought to be and must be, is very difficult. To be hedged about with a dozen or more paid helpers also has its disadvantages for the general secretary. He is denied in large measure the stimulating and enriching personal contacts with the rank and file of men. Furthermore, the presence of a large staff presents another burden, that of training others. Many times it is easier to do a piece of work one's self than to assign it and supervise its being done by another, who may be only a novice. Finally, there is the financial problem to be faced. The local Y. M. C. A. is rarely if ever self-supporting. It must look to the community for from ten to twenty per cent of its funds. It is desirable to keep the membership-fee down, and to let the community share the financial burden; but the one man who must bear the load of this marginal need is the general secretary. He must expect to face this along with the other drawbacks of the secretaryship.

Satisfactions. It frequently happens that the same element in a situation may be to one a hindrance and to another an incentive. The burden of training a staff and a volunteer leadership affords also the privilege of discovering and developing leaders of men. Mining men, who may be diamonds in the rough to become God's leaders, is one of the joys of the Y. M. C. A. secretary. It must not be forgotten, also, that in the present status of the Association movement, the local secretary holds an enviable position of respect and influence. The city of Cleveland was deadlocked in a great street-railway strike. Finally, arbitration being agreed upon, each side to the bitter controversy sought out independently a man to act as third member of the arbitration board. It turned out that both sides had sought the same man, and that man the general secretary of the local Y. M. C. A. Not only is the secretaryship a position of growing esteem, but it is increasingly, for the right man, a permanent career. In 1919 there were no fewer than two hundred secretaries who had been from twenty-five to forty-five years in service.

One of the supreme compensations for any secretary who has been long in service is in seeing boys and men grow into all-round stalwart Christian manhood. To thousands of young men the Y. M. C. A. is home, church, and school. These, mothered by the "Y," the secretary has a unique opportunity to father. To the general secretary there comes also an unusual opportunity to study the relation of Christianity and the church to world problems. To a much greater extent than the church the Y. M. C. A. is thrust out in midstream among the currents of human life, of political, economical, and industrial life. Finally, through his unusual range of activities and his unhampered local independence, the general secretary has an unlimited opportunity for personal growth and for executive and administrative achievement in the field of religious enterprise.

Desirable Qualities. The successful Y. M. C. A. secretary possesses the aggressive qualities of the salesman plus moral earnestness. He should look like a man. He should be friendly, whole-souled, catholic-spirited. He should be systematic and businesslike. He must have a capacity for growth; he must be a team-worker; and he must have what Paul Super calls "the ability to attack and solve," which means initiative and re-sourcefulness. Above all, he must be thoroughly con-secrated to God, completely in love with men, and wholly committed to a Christian purpose. Otherwise he will not stick; he will not always put other men first and himself last, and he will not be what the gen-eral secretary of the Y. M. C. A. must always be "the man behind the men."

The Staff. The staff of the normal-sized city Associ-ation includes secretaries who are specialists in the re-ligious, educational, physical, boys', industrial, social, and employment departments. In addition to these who are connected with the local organization the "staff" of the Y. M. C. A., speaking in a broad sense of the national work, includes also secretaries for county, army and navy, railroad, community, colored, foreign, and student departments. It was the Y. M. C. A. Student Association which fathered the Y. W. C. A. student work, which furnished the background and support for the launching of the Student Volunteer Movement, and which was largely instrumental in the organization of the World's Student Christian Federa-tion. It is that college graduates frequently enter the general secretaryship through the student secretary-ship. Although it is impossible to discuss in detail the work of each of these specialists, three will be consid-ered.

Religious-Work Secretary. The task of the religious-work specialist is to hold meetings of a predominantly religious tone on Sundays and other times in the Association building, in shops, in theatres, or in other places; to promote Bible classes, the reading of religious literature, and personal soul-winning. He secures speakers, plans and advertises meetings, organizes gospel teams, leads prayer meetings, speaks in churches and co-operates with pastors, seeking to link young men with definite church-work. The weekly calendar may include as many as seventy-five Bible classes and fifty religious meetings. Since his work really expresses the soul of the Y. M. C. A. movement, he needs to possess, even more than the general secretary, if that is possible, a passion for soul-winning.

Boys' Work Secretary. This secretary is an expert in boyhood, relating the whole programme of the Y. M. C. A., with proper modifications and adaptations, to the boys of the community. This he does largely through the help of adult leaders and of older boys. The actual schedule of activities includes social events, games and meets, attended by both boys and parents, gymnasium classes, Bible classes, and religious meetings. The boys' work specialist must have the heart of a boy, the head of a man, and the ideals of Jesus Christ.

County Secretary. The development of this type of worker is due to a realization on the part of the Y. M. C. A., which for fifty years centred its activities upon the youth of the cities, that the seven million young men not in cities also need mobilization for Christian purposes. The plan is to bring the programme of the Association home to men and boys in rural counties. Operating from the county-seat as headquarters, the secretary aims to have a local organization or committee in each community, and through home, school, and church, through senior, high-school, and younger boys' groups, and with volunteer leadership, to promote such activities as farmers' institutes, betterment campaigns, gospel teams, get-together events, athletic events, father-and-son banquets, a county convention annually, a boys' conference, and a summer camp. The special qualification for this worker is a sympathy with rural life and a knowledge of rural conditions.

Preparation. "The secretary should have a good common-school education," said the Y. M. C. A. Year-Book for 1892. But times have changed. By 1896 the Association had observed that while only one-fourth of the physical directors and one-seventh of the secretaries were being trained in Association schools, fifty per cent more of these men were remaining in the work than of men not so trained, and their length of service was twice as long. Emphasis was more and more placed upon professional training. Today twenty-five per cent of the secretarial force are college men to begin with. It is also interesting to know that fifty per cent of all "Y" officers employed come from business careers. In the Y. M. C. A., high school or college training plus business experience plus a professional course appears to be the road to success.

There are two Association colleges. The Springfield college offers to high-school graduates a four years' course combining cultural and technical training. The Chicago college offers a three years' cultural and vocational course, which, for those who have graduated from the high school, leads to a diploma; for those who have had two years in college, a professional degree. By arrangement with the University of Chicago, high-school graduates are also offered a five years' course, leading to both a bachelor's degree from the university and a professional degree from the Association college. In both these Y. M. C. A. schools the technical courses include Association science and specialization in the various lines of departmental work, while the more general courses include the Bible, church, psychology, religious education, sociology, economics, biological science, and physical activities. Both colleges offer two-year graduate courses for college graduates.

Fellowship Plan. Other roads lead to the Y. M. C. A. secretaryship. Many local Associations have become "training-centres" where a two years' apprenticeship course is offered for both paid and volunteer workers to be trained and developed for Y. M. C. A. leadership. The general secretary becomes the teacher, leading a secretarial class which meets three times a week from September to June for the study of the organization, history, principles, and method of movement. The principal teaching, however, is done through assigning and supervising "projects." Mr. Super suggests, among others, the following samples in the course of the training of an office secretary: "Call up the directors to notify them of a meeting"; "Deal with a down-and-out visitor"; "Check the laundry in and out." College graduates who are interested in the Y. M. C. A. as a life-work are sometimes given "fellowships;" that is, they are assigned to a local Y. M. C. A. on a small salary to take this two-year course.

The well-developed and effective facilities for training leadership confirm one in the conviction, already formed by a consideration of the scope and significance of the movement in general and of the secretaryship in particular, that the Y. M. C. A. as a vocation requires not merely men, but fit men.

Foreign Secretary. What has already been said about foreign Association work applies here. Y. M. C. A. centres are found throughout the world. There are opportunities for "Y. M. C. A. missionaries" to carry out different phases of the Association programme everywhere.

Statistics. The North American Y. M. C. A. has more than three-quarters of a million members, and more than sixteen hundred fully organized Associations. Its net property and funds paid equal $128,000,000.[1] The total number of employed officers, including all departments, is 5,511, including 312 temporary vacancies.[2] For the ten years, 1909-1919, an average of 111 men were promoted from assistants to executive positions.[3] The annual "turn-over" in the Y. M. C. A. secretaryship is estimated by Mr. C. K. Ober to be about twenty per cent. The secretaryship is a permanent life-work, but it is permanent only for fit men, of whom there is an estimated need for fifteen hundred a year for the next ten years. The salary of a general city secretary of the type considered here varies between $3,500 and $6,000, averaging about $5,000.

---

[1] Y. M. C. A. Year-Book, 1920, Association Press, New York, pp. 110, 111.
[2] Ober, C. K., "Recruiting by Interview," p. 7.
[3] Ober, C. K., "Looking Ahead for Leaders," p. 5.

CHAPTER XI

THE FIELD-SECRETARY

To such wise sayings as that "man is incurably religious," that "man is a social animal," and that "man is a born joiner" might be added this also: that man has a passion for organization. This tendency, which on the whole may be regarded as a mark of wholesome and effective growth and development, was never more pronounced in the field of religion than it is to-day. In considering the work of the "man higher up," in Chapter V., the reader has already been reminded of the extent to which the denominational, interdenominational, local, State, national, and international work of the church is divided and systematized. There are literally scores of boards, departments, divisions, commissions, associations, and societies devoted to furthering various phases of the Christian programme.

Definition. The leaders or executives of these movements, who are, generally speaking, clergymen, have already been taken into account; but there remains to be considered in connection with this type of activity a large group of workers, usually laymen, who are neither national executives nor local officials, and whose chief function is to travel and promote State and national plans and standards among local organizations. This travelling salesman of spiritual goods, who sells and delivers in person, is increasingly known by the name of "field-secretary." There are many workers

157

whose functions of travelling promoter and of head-quarters executive are so evenly balanced that it is impossible to place them. It may be well, therefore, to confine the present discussion rather specifically to those workers designated as "field-worker," "travelling secretary," and "departmental superintendent."

Programme. It is at once evident that the programme to be promoted varies in each case. The Sunday-school worker advances for his department the activities which his State association or denominational board has approved. The Y. W. C. A. field-secretary operates upon a different prospectus; the Y. M. C. A., upon another; the Student Volunteer Movement travelling secretary, another; the Pocket Testament League, another; and so it goes. Aside from these definite distinctions as to measures and methods, however, investigation discloses the fact that in the main, with regard to the routine, the difficulties and advantages, the desirable qualities and preparation, there are surprising similarity and uniformity among these workers. Nevertheless, for the sake of concreteness, the State Christian Endeavor field-secretary is taken as an example; but what is here said will be found to apply to this type of worker in general.

Christian Endeavor is an organization committed to the principle of pledged personal loyalty to Jesus Christ, manifesting itself through Bible-study, prayer, church attendance and support, generous giving, public testimony, and willing and consecrated Christian service. It fosters three kinds of societies, Junior, ages from seven to fourteen; Intermediate, ages from thirteen to nineteen; and Senior, ages eighteen and up. The activities of each society, carried on through many committees, find expression in weekly prayer meetings, monthly business meetings, and church and community undertakings. The organization emphasizes the desirability of bringing boys and girls, young men and women, together under wholesome conditions in mutual social and religious interests. The Christian Endeavor society is a laboratory for the training of Christian character where the ''project method,'' now universally favored, has been long and successfully in operation.

As to special features, the United Society of Christian Endeavor maintains departments of the Quiet Hour, the Tenth Legion, Citizenship, Life-Work Recruits, and Alumni associations. It carries a stock of literature, and the national weekly is *The Christian Endeavor World*. From time to time campaigns are launched extending over stated periods for the accomplishment of definite aims and setting up definite goals.

The special movements within Christian Endeavor and the campaigns are not only carried directly to local societies, but are mediated through county and district unions, which it is a part of the general programme to perfect; and through county, district, State, provincial, and the international conventions. During forty years of continuous growth and increasing usefulness to the church, under the wise leadership of Dr. Francis E. Clark, founder and beloved president, Christian Endeavor has unfolded and perfected a many-sided, comprehensive, unusually adaptable programme, the promotion of which may well challenge the best efforts of the field-secretary.

Routine. The actual schedule of work for the field-secretary varies with the size of the State and the extent and degree of effectiveness of the existing organization. He probably spends from seven to nine months in the field, travelling on an average about ten or fifteen thousand miles annually. While in the field in the course of a week he addresses evening audiences, conducts six or eight conferences, makes from ten to fifteen personal calls upon leaders, and gives two or three high-school assembly talks. Perhaps twice during a month he occupies a pulpit on Sunday. During the entire year, in and out of the field, he averages from one hundred to two hundred letters a month, from three to six articles for publication, and from one to three addresses before denominational gatherings.

Other activities which cannot be so easily tabulated include organizing societies wherever possible, presenting Christian life-work personally at every opening, conferring frequently with State and district committees, assisting often in drafting convention programmes, planning and promoting the State convention, pushing sales of literature at all times, arranging special tours for United Society officers or other leaders, and in many cases editing a State paper. It may be safely affirmed that the dust never settles on a Christian Endeavor field-secretary!

Difficulties. In such a calling difficulties fall thick and fast, the one which stands out most prominently being the so-called "indifference of pastors." Mr. R. A. Walker is perhaps right in suggesting that the fault here rests, at least in part, upon the field-worker, who has failed through wise propaganda and personal contact properly to cultivate the pastor. This shifts the responsibility somewhat, but the situation remains none the less an acute problem, demanding adroit, tactful, courteous, but persistent promotional tactics on the part of the field-secretary.

A second obstacle, scarcely less formidable at the present time, one closely related to the first, finds expression rather vaguely as "misunderstanding of the scope and relation of the movement," or "failure of denominational leaders to co-operate," or "lack of co-ordination." In the last analysis Miss Cynthia Pearl Maus may be right in attributing this to "the overlapping and duplication" in the programmes of the young people's and the church-school movements. On the other hand, this "duplication" may prove more apparent than real. Perhaps a wise adjustment for mutual benefit and for the lasting good of the youth of the church may come about. In the meantime this whole perplexing, unsatisfactory situation presents to all field-workers the very keen personal problem of being fair-minded, of cultivating the capacity to appreciate the good in other movements than one's own, the urgency for extended study and co-operation beyond one's immediate field, and, above all, the necessity of avoiding prejudiced, partisan, and antagonistic attitudes.

Other annoyances must be mentioned briefly. To push plans hard and yet to keep the whole enterprise secondary to the church rather than to allow it to become a substitute for the church, is at once difficult and necessary, for any special movement "comes to an end when it becomes an end in itself." The lack of young men, a difficulty true of the church at large, is frequently mentioned. Financing the movement without antagonizing the church is a more or less perpetual problem, and building balanced convention programmes of help and inspiration year after year is a rare achievement. In addition to the present shortage of leaders a goodly crop of difficulties grows up in every separate field, and, finally, this general question of meeting the increasing absorption of young people with business and social activities, for in all his work with young men and young women the field-secretary must be prepared to face sharp outside competition.

Satisfactions. Again it is true that out of the problems themselves grow the compensations. At least one field-secretary has found his chief satisfaction in successfully relating the programme of his movements with the programme of the church at large. No other religious worker whatever has so abundant and constant opportunity through his broad contacts with local fields and his influence through conventions and conferences to organize and vitalize religious and spiritual forces. He is in a position to render great service to pastors and other leaders in helping to solve local problems. Furthermore, there is among those with whom he works that spirit of youth which says, ''To me all things are possible,'' assuring an enthusiastic and ready responsiveness, always gratifying and stimulating to the leader.

The one greatest joy of the work, perhaps, is the privilege of influencing the life decisions of Christian youth. The field-secretary comes in contact with the most highly selected young persons, who are passing through the most susceptible, significant period of life; and he meets them under the most impressive, advantageous circumstances. Such situations, when not abused or exploited, but judiciously and cautiously taken full advantage of, result in the multiplication many times over of the life of the secretary in permanent Christian decisions and splendid Christian careers. The outstanding glory of Christian Endeavor is its power to inspire lives of Christian service.

Dr. Christine Iverson Bennett, the heroic medical missionary who went out to Basra, in a corner of the Sultan's domain, to give her love and life at "the post of honor," had her first experience in Christian Endeavor in a little town in South Dakota. And she is one of a great multitude of others, ministers, foreign missionaries, and laymen, to whom Christian Endeavor proves the vestibule of Christian life-service.

"Yes, I received my first vision of full-time Christian service at a Christian Endeavor Thanksgiving service." The speaker was Graham Wilson, executive secretary of the West Side Branch of the New York City Y. M. C. A., a man who to-day inspires and directs an organization with eight thousand members, which in one year obtains positions for three thousand men, gives educational instruction to more than four thousand, and provides religious services which have an annual attendance of more than a quarter of a million men. Such a life and influence as that of Graham Wilson is a good illustration of the magnified indirect returns which come from the life-investment of the worker who more than any other promotes such movements as Christian Endeavor.

Desirable Qualities. In this, as in every field of religious work, the first essential is a very definite religious experience on the part of the worker, and the possession of that subtle, pervasive attribute called spirituality. Another qualification which may be assumed is a fair degree of robust health. Clean habits in every particular are about equally indispensable. He should be likable, approachable, sociable, friendly, what Sterling Williams calls "a regular guy," appealing alike to men and women; but he should be also discreet and well poised. He should not be flighty or superficial, but rather one who is able to concentrate on a continuous programme, to think things through, and to carry them out consistently. In just two words, the field-secretary must have judicial enthusiasm. For one who travels on the most impossible schedules, and faces all sorts and conditions of circumstances, the field-worker who carries as part of his equipment a good sense of humor has a decided advantage, to which might be added cheerfulness, resourcefulness, and the capacity for cultivating a habit of succeeding.

Preparation. For any type of field-work a college education is a wise foundation. In addition, in some cases, notably for workers in religious education, specialized training is essential. In all cases practical church-work, with wide experience in volunteer activities, is indispensable. Many field-workers consider business experience as a valuable asset; and, particularly in conservative communities, a theological course or at least Bible training increases one's usefulness and prestige. It goes without saying that one must know from personal contact every phase of the work with which one is to be associated. For the rest, frequent field-workers' conferences, and annual conferences or conventions of the various movements in general, taken in connection with one's actual experiences in the work, furnish good means for continual growth and development. Success as a field-secretary probably depends more upon personality and upon the favorable course of circumstances which open the way for one than upon college diplomas.

Statistics. In this field definite figures can hardly

be presented, because limits are ill defined. Every organized activity of the church may, and probably does, employ "field-workers." Confining discussion to the two movements here considered, the Sunday-school and the Christian Endeavor, it may be estimated that those engaged in the promotional work of the former, under the auspices of the different denominational boards and of the International Sunday-School Association, number about two hundred, of whom no fewer than forty per cent are women. At the present time salaries vary among the workers in the different divisions. They also, of course, vary as between State and denominational workers. There is a movement on foot now[1] which will probably result in an average salary for State Sunday-school workers of about $1,700 to $2,000.

Christian Endeavor field-secretaries probably number not more than twenty-five. Perhaps ten per cent are women. Salaries for interdenominational State workers are between $1,200 and $3,000.

---

[1] From an unpublished report of "the Commission on Salaries," Mr. Walter A. Snow, chairman.

CHAPTER XII

THE DEACONESS

"I commend unto you Phoebe our sister, who is a servant of the church that is at Cenchreae: * * * for she herself hath been a helper of many and of mine own self," wrote Paul, thus furnishing the modern deaconess movement a clew to trace an ancient and honorable descent, and to find sanction in the practice of the primitive church. If in the earliest churches a need for a woman's work had already emerged, one can readily expect to find a greater opportunity and need in the present churches with their more than ten million women members, besides the small children of home and Sunday-school, and with their multiplied schools, societies, guilds, hospitals and homes for young and aged.

Yet the modern deaconess work is very modern indeed. Mrs. Lucy Rider Meyer, who was responsible for its beginning in the Methodist Church, gave up a position as instructor in the Moody Bible Institute in 1886 to start a denominational training-school for city, home, and foreign missionary workers. The following fall her students, who had become absorbed in the community work which had at first been assigned to them as part of their training-course, adopted a distinctive garb, and called themselves "deaconesses." The following year, 1888, the Conference took recognition of the movement, adopting it. The first Methodist deaconesses received an allowance of two dollars a month, clothing, and living. In the spirit of Phoebe a new vocation had been launched, destined to be "a helper of many."

Types of Workers. The Episcopal, as well as the Lutheran, Church has also established deaconess work. In general, whatever be the denomination, the deaconess is "set apart by an appropriate religious service"; wears a distinctive, prescribed attire, and occupies a recognized ecclesiastical position, carrying with it certain regulations, standards, and subjection to stated authority. In other denominations, not recognizing or licensing deaconesses, there are young women carrying on what to a considerable extent may be termed deaconess activities. These, known by such names as "parish worker," "pastor's assistant," "church visitor," "church assistant," "church secretary," and "social secretary," while probably constituting in general a less permanent and less seriously regarded type of vocation, are to be considered as included in the present study.

Programme. "To assist the minister in the care of the poor and sick, the religious training of the young and others, and the work of moral reformation," is, according to Canon 20 of the Protestant Episcopal Church, the duty of the deaconess. This applies primarily in the case of the parochial or local worker, who is usually responsible for club and guild meetings, for organizing the women of the congregation, for educational and relief work, for pastoral work among women, visiting, care of the church fabric, and the oversight of records. There is also, however, the institutional type of work, where the deaconess is in charge of orphanage, home, or hospital; as well as the diocesan or national, where she takes the field in the interest of one or other of the women's organizations or in district educational supervision. Wherever she is, this type of worker is discovering and raising up future leaders for the church; and, in the words of Deaconess Anna G. Newell, her continual concern is "to help the church function for the good of society."

Routine. Consider the pastor's assistant in a city church of a thousand members. Probably five mornings a week she is at the church from ten to half past twelve, busy with conference and correspondence; engaged in special tasks such as making a study of the church-membership, listing the number of vocations represented, telephoning to a dozen people, or sending personal notes of invitation to half a hundred friends of the church to a church dinner, or looking after odds and ends, as when a woman from another town writes the pastor for information about kindergartens for her little girl. The afternoons she spends for the most part in making calls on members, on absentees from Sunday-school and on many others, in addition to the sick. Perhaps she averages twenty-five calls a week. She spends at least three evenings each week at the church, and she attends no fewer than half a dozen society or other group meetings every week, always holding herself in readiness to play for the singing. There is on an average at least one supper a week in the church, at which she plays the part of assistant cook, assistant waitress, and assistant hostess all in one.

Saturday she has a vacation, perhaps, before Sunday, which is her big day. On that day she is on duty practically from nine in the morning until ten at night. She teaches a class in Sunday-school, and attends the

Endeavor meeting in the evening. At the morning and evening services she is no less busy or alert than the pastor himself. She preaches a constant sermon of cheerfulness, friendliness, and Christian sociability.

Difficulties. Being the servant of a church has many trials, particularly when that servant is a woman. In the first place, the restrictions of custom and conservatism, especially in some denominations, hampers a woman of force and initiative, who can gain recognition, influence, and cordial support only by slow and patient achievement. Then, again, she must try to please everybody; that means young and old, men and women, the warm and the cold, deacons and strangers. Only a miracle can prevent misunderstandings, hard feelings, gossipings, jealousies. It is not always easy to meet criticism with smiles, but she must do it. Another problem is to adapt one's personal life, with its physical, mental, and spiritual needs, to the pressing demands of church-work, where each organization always zealously urges its claims for one's support and help.

Another set of disadvantages apply especially to the deaconess. One of these is the question of marriage. At least in the case of the Episcopal deaconess, withdrawal, even for marriage, while not in any way forbidden, is by some regarded as a breach of faith. This sentiment does not apply to the Methodist deaconess. To the latter, on the other hand, belongs especially the problem of financial support, for she receives no salary at all, only a small allowance, which makes this vocation for the girl with dependents practically out of the question. To another distasteful feature, that of wearing a standardized garb, must be added this final drawback, that the deaconess, being always subject to authority, may find heself placed under the leadership of a diffi-cult and uncongenial pastor. She cannot always freely choose her place, nor can she move at will. She is constantly under orders either of the rector of the parish or of the bishop of the diocese. Her modern sister has many things to take into account before following in the steps of Phoebe.

Satisfactions. In like manner as Phoebe, commended unto the Romans by Paul, no doubt found therein a legitimate satisfaction, so the deaconess worker of to-day finds her reward in the knowledge that in rendering service to the poor and needy, the sick and dying, she is re-enforcing the church. For her, opportunities for helpfulness never cease. When Elizabeth Moody, one of the earliest deaconesses in America, an aged veteran of the calling, was asked to state the greatest satisfac-tion which had come to her in her years of work, she smilingly replied, ''I think it was just the continual daily round of usefulness.''

The compensations, of course, vary with the type of work one follows. The deaconess in institutional work, for example, finds her unique recompense in seeing boys and girls grow into strong manhood and womanhood. Who can measure the pride and joy which must come to Deaconess Judson when she recognized in the young couple who one day came to Lake Bluff Orphan-age a boy and a girl whom she had mothered in that same institution and who had now come back to adopt a baby and thus pass on to another generation still the teaching they had there received from her? The work of the parish visitor, to consider another case, is rich in life, contacts and experiences through which, if she have the benefit of a godly pastor's guidance, she comes to understand life and to be equipped and furnished with the power and capacity to counsel, help, and inspire the young people who gradually learn to look to her for leadership. One thus uniformly busy at Christian tasks, as is the deaconess, comes to feel a sense of fellowship with the Saviour, and a harmony with His programme which is its own reward.

Desirable Qualities. "Do you smoke?" "Do you drink?" When a New York pastor propounded these as his first questions to a prospective church visitor he was illustrating the great range and diversity in those personal qualifications which in different times and places may require emphasis. It might be of interest to know that this minister's only concern for this new member of his staff was that she be just wholesome and natural, and that she develop a keen sense of humor. Perhaps the person engaged in deaconess work needs as much as anything a capacity for going more than half-way in meeting and befriending people. She ought to be big-minded, above all suspicion of pettiness. To tact and discretion add patience; to patience, the ability both to co-operate and to lead; and to this, self-discipline and control. As Miss Margaret Eckley, superintendent of the New York Methodist Episcopal Deaconess Association whimsically puts it, the girl who hopes to make a successful deaconess "must have good eyesight for seeing things that need to be done."

Preparation. Although there are exceptions, the standard requirement for a deaconess in both the Methodist and the Episcopal communions is a minimum of high-school training and two years in one of the training-schools for deaconesses. These schools, in addition to courses on the Bible, the organization, doctrine, and history of the church, comparative religions, and missions, offer specialized training in social service, religious education, and secretarial work. Field-work in parish, community, or hospital is usually a part of the curriculum. In some cases, at least in the Methodist Church, a candidate may offer a nurse's training-course in an approved hospital in lieu of the regular training-school requirement. For the lay worker, preparing for some form of deaconess work, there is no standard requirement. A high-school education, stenography, and instrumental music, at least to a fair degree, she needs to have. A course of one or two years in a Bible college is invaluable. In this field with merely makeshift preparation she cannot hope to make an adequate life-work for herself.

Statistics. Methodist and Episcopal deaconesses in the United States number no fewer than twelve hundred. The former receive twenty-five dollars a month and living. The latter receive approximately the same pay that other workers receive for the same services, which amounts for most pastor's assistants, parish visitors, and church assistants to $800 to $1,200 a year, full time. The number of young women engaged in this kind of work, other than the deaconesses referred to, is perhaps not less than fifteen hundred or two thousand.

CHAPTER XIII

THE TEACHER AND SINGER

I. The Director of Religious Education

Religion must be taught. Simply to have caught it no longer suffices. The conviction grows that the church must take the work of education seriously, that the Bible school must be no longer treated as a side-line, that to build Christian character is vital enough to be done well, and that no modern method is too good, no educational standard too high, to be employed in putting Christian ideals, motives, and habits in control of the growing powers of the youth of the land. This conviction awaits fulfillment among twenty million scholars in two hundred thousand church schools in the United States to-day. To whom may these look for the educational leadership of the church?

Programme. The answer to this question is, The director of religious education. This professional worker may be a clergyman, a deaconess, or a layman. He is *not* assistant pastor, church assistant, or all-round handy man. He is, on the contrary, a specialist who substitutes scientific management for slack methods in an enterprise which until recently has been notoriously clumsy, amateurish, and ineffective. In general his work may be divided into the administrative and the promotional.

173

Considering the latter, he first of all co-operates with the denominational office, adapting and putting through national programmes. Locally he co-operates with other church schools and with interdenominational agencies for union institutes and other union plans. Within his own community he influences, modifies, and correlates those agencies which bear on the life of his own school. Within his own church he controls and unifies all organizations which are educational. He keeps religious education foremost, and, in the words of Richardson, "he creates educational idealism."

Within the church school the director is the chief administrative officer. He supervises aim, method, curriculum; he observes classes in session; he reorganizes departments; he shifts teachers; he standardizes enrolment and promotion; he maintains a balanced programme; he administers the school in such a way as to conserve time, interest, and energy. Yet he is not an autocrat. By introducing system and consistent purpose he rather substitutes law and order for arbitrariness. The director of religious education usually himself conducts the teacher-training class. Because this vocation is just finding itself, there is no routine into which the worker steps.

Difficulties. The director of religious education has an unusually hard place to fill. The position would be a trial if for no other reason than that it is in a new field, lacking standards, recognition, and permanence. The director's position will be what he makes it and nothing more. He has an unusually keen anxiety to succeed. Quick results are expected of him; but in the work of education results come slowly at best, slower still when one must depend upon teachers and officers who can only gradually be brought up to the measure of the expert. His relation to the congregation and to the pastor is an uncertain quantity.   The former, lacking information and knowledge, fails to support his efforts as it should; while the minister, although wholly unqualified to do so, may assume to dictate to him, or may insist upon using him in the capacity of assistant pastor.   A far more serious problem than any of these has to do with the fact that the specialist in religious education has almost inevitably adopted a standard of values and a conception of religious training which brings him into conflict with the conservatives of his constituency.   For example, he is almost certain to believe that Christian living and not Christian creeds should be the centre of the curriculum; and, holding that all of life is a part of the book of God's revelation, he may offer in his course of study a few pages less of the Bible and a few pages more of life than will suit some.   Thus not only the newness of the work, and the ignorance of the church, and the slowness of results, but even the current changing tendencies in curriculum-making as well, add to the worries of the director of religious education.

Compensations.   So long, however, as the emphasis continues to shift to education as the sure foundation for bringing in the democracy of God among men, the satisfaction of the worker in the field of religious education must outweigh his difficulties.   However thickly beset with problems he may be, he has always the joy of knowing that he is fighting at a strategic point in the Christian enterprise.   He has large opportunity for constructively influencing social progress, both for making society Christian and for making Christianity social.

He has the fine happiness of seeing "youngsters blossom from short pants into Christian manhood," as Dr. Hugh Hartshorne puts it; and these products of the modern church school go forth not only stamped on the cover with the label "Christian," but with Christian motives and habits woven into the very fibre and muscle of their being. In short, there is no reward which may be claimed by any teacher of youth which this leader may not claim, with this addition: that, while public-school teachers are primarily concerned with imparting "tools," the religious educator specializes primarily in imparting character.

Desirable Qualities. The successful director of religious education must be a rare personality. He needs to possess an unusual combination of qualities. He must have a genius for organization and for detail, while at the same time having a broad vision and a capacity for promoting not only organization but inspiration. He must be a good manager of people, both as individuals and in groups; for he is not a driver, but a leader. He must be able to get along with people; and at the same time he must be independent, and self-reliant enough to get along without people, too. He must not be inclined to be dictatorial or dogmatic or superficial or hasty. Indeed, at one and the same time he must be diplomat, executive, and "consecrated, skilled, prophetic, contagious teacher.'"

Preparation. The leader in this area must have a college education plus. Although the field is wide and new and unorganized, the actual opportunities for this

---

[1]Richardson, Norman E., "Religious Education as a Vocation," Northwestern University, Evanston, Illinois, 1920.

type of work are largely limited to the larger city churches, which are apt to place a premium upon adequate preparation. The Religious Education Association recommends that he should have a graduate course leading to the A.M. degree. There are about fifty or more colleges in the United States now offering special courses in religious education of the kind deemed desirable. These include such general subjects as educational psychology, the philosophy of education, supervision of teaching, and such others as the history of Christian education, the theory of religious education, the organization and administration of the church school, curriculum-making, and practice or field-work. Such graduate work takes one year and probably two years. One who expects to step into the leadership of the present advance movement to make religious education real education and to pose as "the educational pastor" of a church must know what he is about.

Statistics. The exact number of directors of religious education is not available. A recently published list contained the names of 131, of whom fifty-three were laymen, forty-seven ordained, and thirty-one were women. Others are entering this field rapidly, and this list is only partial, indicating in general the present situation. It is significant that among the calls of the mission boards are thirteen for Sunday-school specialists. The salary is about $3,000.

II.   THE MISSION-SCHOOL TEACHER

"I was born in a little log cabin sixteen by eighteen feet in the hills of East Tennessee. * * * We had a large family, and we usually had company. * * * Sometimes, if we wanted to turn around, we would almost have to go out and turn around, and then come back into the house. * * * My mother did not realize that I was a child. * * * She made a little old woman of me. * * * At the age of seven I began cooking * * * and took care of the babies. * * *

"My father made moonshine whiskey. * * * We drank from the time I can remember until I was sixteen. My mother left us when I was fourteen. I was housekeeper, sister, and mother * * * , sewing, cooking, washing, ironing, milking. * * * Father * * * drank continually. Whenever there was a drunken crowd or frolic, he went and we girls went, too.

"I heard of a Presbyterian school. * * * I borrowed ten dollars and went. * * * I stayed three and one-half years. * * * During vacations I worked in lumber-camps and a hotel. * * * Besides helping myself through school I kept one of my brothers in school. * * * I was offered a scholarship to go to college. But I decided that I ought to come home and try to give the other children in the community an opportunity to get an education."

Programme. This extract from the "Life of a Mountain Girl, Written by Herself,'" may fittingly serve as the background for the home-mission work, not only in the Southern mountains, but also among the Alaskans, negroes, Indians, and Mexicans, a work which employs physicians, nurses, matrons, and community workers as well as teachers. With certain definite modifications, what is here said of the latter worker may be taken in a general way to include these other types of vocation also.

---

[1]Published by the Woman's Board of Home Missions, Presbyterian Church in the U. S. A., New York.

The fundamental policy of the mission school is to reach the individual, and through the individual to reach the community; to give the individual a useful, Christian training in order through him to help develop a useful, Christian community. The schooling offered, therefore, is not calculated to educate one away from his own people, but to educate him for them, to inspire him with a Christian motive for service, and to send him forth an effective farmer, teacher, home-maker, industrial, or commercial worker. The courses of study are practical and vocational. In addition to principals, superintendents, rural supervisors, and general teachers of grade and high-school subjects, there are teachers specializing in such subjects as domestic science and arts, music, Bible, kindergartens, primary, industrial, gymnasium, physical education, manual training, and weaving. There are both boarding and day schools, including all grades from the kindergarten to the fourth year of the high school.

Routine. Take the life of an English teacher in a boarding-school which offers eight grades, beginning with the fourth and running through the fourth year of the high school. Perhaps there are 150 pupils. Her pupils come to her in groups of ten. Class hours are from nine to four. Out of school she takes girls on hikes and outings; in the evening she reads aloud, or superintendents "social evenings" with their games and programmes; or, if it be her turn, she supervises the evening study-hour. For a month or two each school year she directs the weekly religious meeting, which may perhaps take the form of a Christian Endeavor society. She may live permanently or for a limited period in the "model cottage,'' the home where the girls in alternate groups come to reside six weeks for a life-demonstration of Christian home-making. Boarding-school life for this teacher, as for all others, is largely a continuous, community affair. Her daily lesson plan must include the whole day and the whole school. In the teacher all activities largely centre. As Miss Mabel M. Sheibley expresses it, there is hardly an event, an inspiration, an undertaking, in which ''there is not usually a teacher somewhere at the top or the bottom of it.''

Difficulties. One of the very greatest problems which the teacher faces is this constant demand upon her time and drain upon her nervous energy. Then too, mission-school life presents a steady routine without the relief of outside interests. There is monotony; there is hard work; there is little leisure. She faces empty lives into whom she must be forever pouring herself without having at hand those fresh, stimulating contacts upon which to replenish her own store. There are actual hardships, also, of a very real nature, to be endured in the out-of-the-way, poorly equipped mission-school. Think of the unpleasant situation of a school which, in the long rainy season, finds itself fairly set in the mud, where the teachers can not come down-stairs without wearing their rubbers!

Compensations. In teaching those who are in the greatest need of education, those who are the most eager to get it, and those who respond most quickly to it, the teacher finds her delight. She teaches not those who come grudgingly, forced, maybe, by a truancy law. No, her scholars are willing to mortgage their future to get a chance to come, or, like one girl, to pick berries from morning till night, week in and out, to pay her annual tuition fee, perhaps seventy-five dollars. The teacher's inspiration comes in seeing these children, who come from almost nothing in home conditions develop so rapidly that the improvement can almost be seen from day to day. When a pupil who came from a squalid hut goes back to make a Christian home; when a youth, who earned his way through school, denies himself the opportunity of a college scholarship in order to go back home to teach and to send others to school, the teacher realizes that she makes a better investment than the putting by of much money in the bank. She lays up capital in hearts and heads, live investments which go forth on swift feet to earn for her compound interest.

Character and Training. In addition to the characteristics desirable in any teacher the worker in the mission-school needs an unlimited amount of consecration, love of children, and adaptability. She must have a smile for the time when the plumbing goes wrong, when there is nothing but snow for a week, and when the well goes dry. Above everything else, she, too, must be a youngster in spirit and in sympathy. Any one possessing these qualifications and a normal-school or college diploma, or three or four years of successful teaching experience in addition to a high-school diploma, and who is a church-member, and brings a letter of recommendation from her pastor, may find a place waiting for her on the staff of a mission school.

Statistics. Among the laymen sent out in the home field by the mission boards the teachers described in this section are perhaps the predominant type of workers.

There are probably no fewer than fifteen hundred young women in such positions in the United States. Twenty-two is about the average age of entering this vocation, and the salary is $450 to $600, with board and laundry. In this field the boards are calling for ninety-six women and six men. Other calls which may well be referred to at this point are for women to do evangelistic work, fifty-three; nurses, forty-nine; medical workers, seven; and workers for special groups, not ordained workers, eleven women and twenty-six men.

III. The Singing Evangelist

A blind Scotsman once wrote a sermon which has never ceased being preached around the world over and over again. Countless thousands have repeated it. Multitudes love it. No one can estimate how many lives it has cheered, or how many souls it has warmed and strengthened. The man was George Matheson and his sermon a sermon in song, "O Love that wilt not let me go."

That music and religion are inseparable is indicated by the permanent and rich hymnology of the church. Music is the very breath of religion. Worship is not only an attitude of the will and an exercise of the intellect, but a feeling of the heart as well; and sacred song is one of God's swiftest messengers to the human heart. Scattered through the pages of a little booklet containing testimonials from recent converts were found no fewer than eighteen quotations from standard hymns. Saved men have gospel songs woven into their hearts; and nobody knows how many souls are lifted heavenward on the gentle wings of persuasive song. Charles Alexander said that a song may be "a sermon on wheels."

Programme. The opportunity for full-time salaried workers in the field of church music, however, is not large. There are many organists, soloists, choristers, and singers who find part-time employment; but in the main the largest opening for religious work in music is that afforded in the vocation of "singing evangelist," by which is meant one, ordinarily a layman, who co-operates with the evangelist in the conduct of revival meetings, assuming full responsibility for the music. For the present purpose a small number of pianists are assumed to be included. In general the singing evangelist's schedule will include the leading of the congregational singing, the singing of solos at practically every service, and organizing and conducting a choir. He is also expected to enter heartily into the spirit and work of the meeting as a whole. Soul-winning is his goal as much as it is that of the evangelist. During the meeting he makes calls and does personal work constantly. One should read in connection with this section, Part I, chapter IV.

Problems and Satisfactions. The singing evangelist shares largely in the fortunes and misfortunes of the evangelist. If he has a distinctive problem, it is, probably, to face a certain lack of appreciation. He serves always in a subordinate position in relation to the evangelistic enterprise as a whole, and he must, therefore, fit his plans into those of others. His unique compensation comes in the joy which he brings through song to saved and unsaved alike. He is ever helping people to "pack up their troubles" and to "brighten the corner where they are."

Desirable Qualities. First of all, the singing evangelist must be humble rather than egotistic. He must be thoroughly Christian, willing to see himself decrease in order that the work may increase. He must have that truly missionary capacity for getting along well with others. He must be morally in earnest, not easily offended, and not given to stunts and slang. As Mr. W. E. M. Hackleman phrases it, ''he must be in the work because he can't be happy out of it,'' and not to exhibit his own good voice, which he is assumed to possess, or to make money, or to sell books.

Preparation. If the candidate is not a college graduate, and intends to enter this calling as a life-work, he should at least have a year or two of a religious worker's course in a good Bible college. Personal work and general contacts make this desirable. His special musical training should include in addition to voice-culture musical theory, composition, conducting, and hymnology. The Interdenominational Association of Evangelists admits singing evangelists and pianists to membership, the requirement for admission being at least two years of actual work and at least twenty lessons in voice from a competent teacher.

Statistics. Probably no fewer than two hundred persons are employed more or less regularly as singing evangelists in the United States. Of these about twenty per cent are women. The income varies from $1,500 to $3,000 a year.

CHAPTER XIV.

THE SOCIAL-RELIGIOUS WORKER

The American city, which now shelters more than half the total population of the United States, presents a complex, difficult problem. It possesses both the best and the worst elements of civilization. Its schools, churches, libraries, hospitals, art, literature, music, parks, avenues, buildings, refined society, reservoirs, electric lights, and rapid transit embody the finest achievements of the race; but its congestion, ignorance, want, exploitation, graft, vice, immorality, disease, commercialized amusements, lawlessness, abandon, and disregard of others constitute the greatest menace to personality, to neighborliness, to righteous living, and to the democracy of God.

The trouble is that the city has grown too fast and too big. Greater New York City contains as many people as eight far western States; some people are still living who were born when Chicago was a town of only eleven thousand. In handling this ever-increasing population the physical facilities of the city have far outdistanced its social and spiritual facilities. The mechanics of city living are well perfected; but the humanities of life, the measures for preserving the sanctity of the home, the sacredness of personality, and the ideals of the group, for assimilating and adapting each newcomer personally and completely to the community, these are far behind in development. Just as long as builders can excavate deeper, skyscrape higher, and pack in tighter, people continue to be dumped into the city until as many as four thousand exist in a single block, and the problem of maintaining privacy, decency, home life, and high standards of living, thinking, and behaving becomes increasingly acute.

When people live in crowds, it becomes a habit not to see the trees for the forest. That is why in some respects the great modern city is a new kind of wilderness, surprisingly lonely, where people frequently lose their way, and faint, and perish by the way unnoticed. It is not uncommon in New York for people to die in their rooms and not be missed until their bodies are discovered days afterward; or for very small children, whose mothers toil away for the day, to forage on the street for all the food they get during the day, like four-year-old Esther, of whom Miss Bertha Merrill of the Disciples' Community House speaks, who died from poisoning from food picked up on the street. The conditions which such cases as these illustrate are found most conspicuously in New York or Boston, but to a larger or less extent they apply to certain sections of all the large cities from coast to coast.

Definition. Thus it is that, whereas, in Livingstone's day missionary pioneering was confined largely to the unexplored continent, to-day it centres increasingly in the unsocialized city, where people by hundreds of thousands and millions form swamps and marshes of humanity. This new field of social service is wide. A recent list of social agencies[1] includes no fewer than

---

[1] Lattimore, Eleanor L., "Social Agencies," Industrial Commission, Y. W. C. A.

150 different organizations for social betterment, including such familiar ones as the Red Cross, the Associated Charities, the Travellers' Aid, the Russell Sage Foundation, the National Consumers' League, the Review of Motion Pictures, the Parent-Teacher Association, the Public Health Service, the Rockefeller Foundation, milk stations, the Child Welfare Association, the day-nursery, the Big Brother Movement, the Boy Scouts, the Camp-fire Girls, the Playground Association, and federal, State, and special immigration and Americanization activities. Strictly speaking, however, these enterprises in general are not the legitimate field for the religious worker as such. For the purpose in hand, which is to describe "church careers" suitable for Christian Life-Work Recruits, the social-religious worker may be defined as one who, with a primary religious motive, carries on social service in the employ of an organization which is definitely religious.[1]

Types of Work. In a sense the whole programme of the church at home and abroad is social service. Dr. John McDowell regards social service as "a function of religion rather than a department." From this point of view, to a greater or less extent, minister, foreign missionary, deaconess, and lay worker all do work of this type. Especially is this true of the programme of the home missionary, the overseas worker, the Association secretary, and the deaconess. However, the following are more specifically social-religious workers.

The Migrant-Group Worker. In an interesting leaflet called "Harvesting Souls in Berry-Patches" Miss

---

[1]Definition suggested by Miss Adelaide T. Case, Department of Religious Education, Teachers' College, Columbia University.

Lila B. Acheson describes the work which home-mission boards are just beginning to take up among the groups of harvesters who for weeks and months, uprooted from normal home and community conditions, migrate from south to north with the season. These people find themselves without educational, social, and religious opportunities of any kind. The programme to be undertaken is still a matter of experiment, but it will undoubtedly include such features as a kindergarten for the small children, supervised play, wholesome entertainment, and some forms of Sunday and week-day religious services.

The Community-Station Worker. This worker finds employment under home-mission boards in backward communities, in "the back washes of life's rush," where school and church have not yet entered. The community-station worker is neither teacher nor preacher, but he prepares for both school and church by nursing into life a community consciousness, by setting up a programme of community-betterment, and by developing leadership through group activities and clubs. The programme of such a worker includes many activities, from getting acquainted with every one for a mile around, nursing the sick, and conducting a Sunday-school or Christian Endeavor society to superintending the building of a bridge across Cutshin Creek, as did Miss Rose McCord, of Wooton, Ky.

The Colporteur. This worker is more than simply a distributer of religious literature. He is a missionary in very real way, who canvasses foreign colonies and settlements. In addition to doing personal soul-winning he frequently gathers valuable information which may lead to the establishment of permanent mission work. The consecrated written page has always been an effective preacher and evangelist, and just as literature is coming to the front in missionary enterprise overseas, Christian literature translated into the language of their native lands is proving successful in reaching and influencing the Bohemians, Italians, Hungarians, Ukrainians, Poles, Russians, and Jews here. There is at present a plan to establish a training-school offering a two years' course for this type of worker.[1]

I.   THE COMMUNITY-HOUSE WORKER

Programme. Under this heading may be listed in general at least three types of workers. 1. Practically any member of the staff of a socialized or institutional church who, using the church as a base, mediates the Christian message within the immediate community to all without regard to church affiliations. 2. Any member of the staff of a settlement or community house located within a congested area of foreign population to carry on a programme of Americanization. 3. The worker in a similar centre located within an industrial area. The following study of a worker of the second type mentioned has in the main many points in common with the others.

Community work is a labor of love. The purpose of the community-house worker is to Christianize the community through ministering to its needs, with emphasis upon the last four words, "ministering to its needs." "Americanization with a religious background" is another way of saying the same thing.

---

[1]See "Evangelizing the Immigrant," pamphlet, issued by the Missionary Department, Presbyterian Board of Publication and Sabbath-School Work, Philadelphia, Penn.

Here are immigrants, parents and children, who first of all must be taught the English language in order to be taught American traditions, ideals, and standards. A community worker is a foreign missionary to "Little Italy," who goes a stranger to dwell among strangers, to make them realize through his life that God cares. To get acquainted with people as individuals, to make a real friend of every one of them, to break barriers of class and race, to approximate the redeeming spirit of neighborliness, to make society a safe place for saving souls rather than trying directly to save them, all this is the programme of Christian-community work. Diffendorfer[1] well states the fundamental policy of the movement when he speaks of the opportunity of the church, "not to build up itself out of the community, but to build up the community out of its very life."

Routine. Consider a community worker on the East Side, New York City. She is the senior member of a staff of three full-time and seven part-time workers. She divides responsibility for the whole enterprise with a man who is in charge of the work for men and boys. The "parish" lies within a radius of about two blocks, now having contacts with between four hundred and five hundred children and grown-ups, representing thirteen nationalities. The weekly schedule of activities which she supervises includes a cooking-class of ten, a sewing-class of twenty-four, a millinery class of sixteen, a story-telling hour on Saturday afternoon, and the kindergarten. Other activites include fre-

---

[1]Diffendorfer. Ralph E., "The Church and the Community," Interchurch World Movement, 1920, p. xxi.

quent evening entertainments, a chorus class, private music-lessons on the piano, manual training, gymnasium, and Sunday-school.

This worker keeps daily office-hours from ten to one or two to five. Perhaps three evenings a week she spends at the centre. In the course of a day, in addition to the stated tasks, she shops for the noonday meal, buys and prepares the material for the cooking, sewing, or millinery class, interviews one or two mothers, makes three or four calls, prescribes for one woman whom she finds ill, plans the menu and invites the guests for a "mothers' dinner," which the girls in the cooking-class will cook and serve, and, in all that she undertakes or starts, she suffers a dozen interruptions from unexpected sources, as, for example, when a small boy comes rushing in, whose face an older sister has washed with lye! One readily agrees with Miss Bertha Merrill when she smilingly remarks that "the best preparation for a community worker is to have been raised as the oldest child in a large family."

Difficulties. One of the chief problems of the community worker is to achieve common understanding. To get past the obstacle of language is not easy; but, where a medium of mutual ideas and traditions and outlook on life is lacking, the situation is still less easy. The worker meets misunderstanding, suspicion, and prejudice. Furthermore, practically all the work of the community centre represents high-tension activity. The groups worked with, lack homogeneity. In age, in race, in creed, in refinement, in spirit, the few persons gathered in one class may represent polar extremes. Problems of interest and of discipline are thus doubly hard and exacting. There is a lack of stability and certainty which is also trying. It is impossible to anticipate the response to any proposal. The future is always an unknown quantity, especially where it is estimated that a third of the constituency changes every six months. Added to this is the undisputed fact that in terms of evangelization or gain in church-membership community work is of all types the slowest in results. Direct appeals for the Christian church are not made. The Christian motive and zeal of the worker find expression principally in example, in spirit, and in creating a Christ-like atmosphere at the community house, calculated to fulfil its own subtle mission in the hearts of many who come. And it is exactly the maintenance of this essential Christian atmosphere which is perhaps the greatest problem of the community worker.

Satisfactions. After so formidable a catalogue of disadvantages one might think rewards must be entirely lacking, but for the person really on fire to serve there are just as many gratifications as there are contacts, for every personal contact in the community parish spells an opportunity to help some one who is inadequately adjusted, groping in the dark, toward a fuller, more abundant life. The comparative responsiveness of the children, their eagerness to please, their quickness to learn, and their ready co-operation in gaining entree to the homes are among the real satisfactions of the worker. To get to know people intimately and to find that beneath the racial name and the alien skin beats a heart as human and as true as any is a rare experience of personal growth. The handiest place to make a trip around the world is in the settlement work of a large American city. It is a training-school for world citizenship; and, best of all, it is a place where one may practise daily lessons from Him who said, "I came not to be ministered unto, but to minister."

Desirable Qualities. "An open mind, a sympathetic heart, and a willing hand" are exactly the prerequisites for the successful community worker. An open mind means the capacity to expect to find, to find, and to appropriate the good in others. One who expects to do social service should not expect to find people who are hopelessly depraved, entirely unenlightened, or dressed in rags and tatters. When the present writer asked his debating-class at the "Labor Temple" in the east side of New York City, composed of young men and women, to mention subjects for debate which would interest them, the suggestions included "Platonic Friendship," "the Income Tax," "Capital Punishment," "Eugenics," "Compulsory Military Training," and "Plato's Republic"! Broad sympathy, patience, an even temper, and a good sense of humor are fine assets, to which may be added in anticipation of the many diversified demands a ready adaptability.

Preparation. Successful community work is a science. It cannot succeed on sentiment. The least training with which one should attempt full responsibility for community work is a full college course and graduate work of at least one year. An increasing number of colleges are offering courses for social-religious workers, which include such studies as education, immigrant problems, industrial conditions and relations, modern social problems, psychology of the Christian life, hygiene, nursing, household arts, and supervision of recreation, as well as elementary courses in the Bible calculated to give "a working knowledge of the social teachings of Jesus." This graduate work can well be taken over a period of two to three years, in connection with actual community work, on a part-time basis.

Statistics. No doubt thousands of people are engaged in social-service work in the United States today. When the area is limited by the definition adopted in these pages, however, and further narrowed to the activities of workers representing the Protestant evangelical churches, the number is probably between six hundred and eight hundred, of whom perhaps seventy-eight per cent are women. For the type of work described here, the salary is $1,800 to $2,500. The mission boards have openings for more than two hundred women settlement workers now.

II.   The Salvation Army Officer

Purpose. The Salvation Army was born to William and Catherine Booth in a gospel tent in the East End of London in 1865. It was consecrated to the proclamation of the gospel of Christ to all men, but especially to the common people of the great cities, untouched by ordinary religious efforts. It is an evangelical religious organization, which has but three words in its theology: Salvation for self, for others, for the world; Love for the lost; and Service on the part of those who realize "that they must now live for Him who died for them." It is "the Church of the Lost," which to-day throughout the world lives for one purpose—to bring salvation to the slums and the streets.

Organization. The Army has a closely knit military system, at the bottom of which is the corps, which is the smallest local unit. These may number one or more in any city. Above the corps are divisions, and above these in turn is the territory, the usual national unit for the work. Above the national work is the general, or commander-in-chief, with the international headquarters in London. In the United States are three territories united into a National Command under the leadership of Commander Evangeline Booth, a daughter of the founder. The officers, beginning with the lowest, are lieutenant, captain, ensign, adjutant, and commandant. Above these are the staff officers, ranging from captain, major, brigadier, colonel, commissioner, to chief of staff and general. All of these are full-time salaried workers, but below them are the soldiers or regular lay members, who, at a minimum age of fifteen, are sworn in by a service under the "blood-and-fire flag," and are subject also to military orders and regulations.

Activities. The largest single social relief organization in the world is perhaps the Salvation Army. Under its two departments of evangelistic and social work it carries on a varied programme, including hotels, industrial institutions, labor bureaus, rescue homes, prison work, children's homes, maternity homes, slum posts, nurseries, summer fresh-air camps, and even distribution of coal and ice. All of this work it carries on for all people in need, regardless of race, color, or creed. The department of army and navy work holds religious services and establishes Homes. Young people receive regular instruction in the Bible. There is a corps cadet brigade for youth looking forward to officers' careers, and also "Life-Saving Guard" organizations for both boys and girls, which have as their motto, "Save your body; save your mind; save your soul; save others."

Method. The method of the Army is to go out into the highways and persuade them to come in. Meetings are held on the streets everywhere when lawful, and, when weather permits, throughout the year. These meetings are followed by a parade to the indoor meeting which follows. These are always intensely evangelistic in spirit and tone. Members are urged to attend all meetings, to contribute systematically weekly, and to seek every opportunity to testify and pray in the meetings. Daily Bible-reading, family prayers, personal soul-saving, are emphasized. Dr. Francis E. Clark has said this about the Salvation Army: "It sticks to first principles. It believes what it believes with all its heart; and thus, drawing power from on high, it is able, with one hand in God's, with the other to lift the fallen, however low they may have sunk."

Desirable Qualities and Training. In the evangelistic work emphasis is upon ability in speaking, singing, organizing, and mixing. In the social work it is on large sympathies, good management, resourcefulness, and energy. In a general way it may be said that any person who is conscious of a personal saving religious experience, who is young and healthy, "willing to adapt himself to any work and to work hard," has a place waiting for him on the staff of the Army. After appearing for an examination as to one's motives and conviction of a "call" the successful candidate is sent to one of the training-schools, of which there are two in

New York and two in Chicago, for nine months, receiving tuition and living free. At the end of that time he or she is commissioned as lieutenant and sent into the field.

The curriculum of the Salvation Army training-college is intensely practical. It includes teaching in the Bible, with emphasis upon evangelism and soul-saving; lectures by Army officers and leaders; training in Salvation Army doctrine and discipline; and music. "Side classes" include a project in corps work in which each cadet, the name given the student officers, prepares a weekly regulation report for an imaginary corps of which he is in command; platform work; first aid; missionary information; general education where needed; and domestic economy for the girls.

Statistics. Salvation Army officers, especially those of lower rank, are very poorly paid. Lieutenants are supposed to receive thirteen dollars a week. After two years they are promoted to the rank of captain, and receive fourteen dollars a week. After five years they become ensign; and after another five years adjutant. Above this advancement is by selection. The officers and cadets of the Army in the United States number 3,649, of whom about sixty per cent are women.[1]

III. THE RESCUE-MISSION WORKER

Statistics. The type of worker to be considered in this section probably numbers no fewer than 250 in the United States. The salary is about $1,200 or $1,500 and in many cases living.

---

[1] Information kindly furnished by Colonel J. E. Margetts, of the National Headquarters.

Programme. The community worker is one sent to redeem the neighborhood; the Salvation Army officer is one sent to redeem the street; the rescue-mission superintendent is one sent to redeem the down-and-outer. The last-named worker is truly a fisher of men, who lowers his net far out in the black, deep sea of sin. The whole platform of the rescue-mission movement is the salvation of sinners through faith in Jesus Christ. Character-rehabilitation is its sole purpose. It considers any man with breath in his body worth saving, and its policy is never to give a man up. Thus in the large city it usually stands as the last stop on the way to suicide and utter wreck. In a sense, this type of work is wholly evangelistic, because its work of feeding, clothing, and sheltering is always secondary to the gospel meeting and personal soul-winning. This reclamation of human wastage is high service to society. The corner-stone of the rescue mission is this: that ''a redeemed world can be made only by the redemption of the character of men through the Christ of the cross.''

Desirable Qualities and Preparation. The rescue-mission superintendency is perhaps the most highly selective of all the types of religious vocation. Simply to say that the superintendent should be completely self-controlled, friendly, good-natured, earnest, sympathetic, tolerant, consumed with a love for men, and thoroughly saturated with a God-given patience is to overlook the chief qualification, which seems to be that he himself should be a redeemed outcast, one who, himself, ''broken and bruised and sore, has cried at His open door.'' Curiously enough, it is by way of the saloon that some of the greatest rescue-mission workers have come.

As to preparation of the kind given by theological schools and colleges, there seems to be a danger of over-education rather than the reverse. To be genuinely converted, to study the Scriptures, to be taught by the Holy Spirit, and to develop gradually into responsibility through an apprenticeship of volunteer service in the mission itself, remains probably the best training for the superintendent of the rescue mission. Of the converts of the McAuley Mission who have entered religious vocations more than half are rescue-mission workers.

Difficulties. The vocabulary of these twice-born men has no place for the word "hardships." Yet it is not all sunshine even here in this atmosphere perpetually glowing with religious fervor and love. There are no office-hours, or, rather, all hours are office-hours in a rescue mission, for the superintendent is subject to all calls all the time. It is a wearing and tearing job to which, as Superintendent John H. Wyburn expresses it, "you must give your life-blood all the time or quit." Perhaps the hardest cross is the ingratitude of the rank and file of men who, coming and going in an endless line, misunderstanding, spurning, and scorning, unfeeling and dumb like water-soaked logs adrift, place a continual strain on the worker's patience and long-suffering.

Satisfactions. The joy of the rescue-mission superintendent comes through being a co-worker with God, through finding now and again real gold hidden away in the crushed human clay which he handles, and through witnessing with his own eyes the modern miracles performed by the "down-swooping, uplifting power of the gospel of Jesus Christ." It must be compensation immeasurable for the superintendent when he hears from his children in Christ such words as these:

"I came to this mission as a homeless man. I had been through all the rough stuff. I came homeless, friendless, ragged, and drunk. I've never been the same man since I got up from that bench."

* * *

"As I came down the Bowery to-night, I passed the saloon where I spent many years of my life. I thanked God for planting my feet on higher ground; and I pray He will plant me so high that I can never fall."

* * *

"I thank God for this mission. I was led here through prayer. Prayer is a wonderful thing, but you've got to keep your mind on it and pray hard. I was raised as a Christian, went to church and Sunday-school; but I knew nothing of a personal Saviour until I came here."

* * *

"I've been about as good a booze-fighter as they make 'em. When I got so low nothing could help me, I met a man who knew Jesus. The best friend I have to-night is the Lord Jesus."

* * *

"Three years ago the fourteenth of June I sat in Madison Square, broke in money and health, thrown out of every place. When the cop made me get off the park, where could I go? No place but the mission of Jesus, where I have many times sat and sneered and scoffed. Now I have health and happiness. I had bucked the line since I was eighteen, chain-gang and all. Only Jesus could keep me. I'm proud to say, thank God, Jesus saved me!''

* * *

''I thank God for four weeks and three days of peace and happiness.''

* * *

''I want to thank God for another day, for four weeks and three days of life.''

* * *

''I am thankful to be here to-night and to testify that three years, ten months, and fourteen days ago I gave my heart to Jesus. Do you see that motto over the door? 'No Compromise with Sin.' That is my slogan, for, if I took my eyes off Jesus Christ, I'd be in the gutter again to-morrow.''

* * *

Is it any wonder that the superintendent of that mission,[1] at the close of such a service could say, with his face radiant, ''I marvel anew every day at the keeping power of God''? and testimonies like these are given three hundred and sixty-five nights and fifty-two Sundays every year in a rescue mission.

---

[1]Between the date when he invited the writer to dinner and to spend an evening at the mission and the writing of this manuscript Superintendent Wyburn, of the McAuley Water Street Mission has passed on, still safe in ''the keeping power'' of God.

REFERENCES

PART III

GENERAL

a. Eastman, E. Fred, "Unfinished Business," Presbyterian Board of Publication, Philadelphia, 1921.

b. Thompson, Charles L., "The Soul of America," Fleming H. Revell Company, New York City, 1919.

c. Ward, Harry F., "The New Social Order," Macmillan & Company, New York City, 1919.

CHAPTER X

d. Wilson, Eliz., "Fifty Years of Association Work," National Board, Y. W. C. A., New York City, 1916.

e. Super, Paul, "Training a Staff," Associated Press, New York City, 1920.

f. Soares and Ober, "Y. M. C. A. Secretaryship," Association Press, New York City, 1919.

g. Mayo, "That Damn Y," Houghton, Mifflin Co., Boston, 1920.

CHAPTER XI

h. "Organized Sunday-school Work in North America," 1914-18, International Sunday-school Association, Chicago, 1918.

CHAPTER XII

i. Tippy, Worth M., "The Socialized Church," Chapters VII, VIII, Eaton and Mains, New York City, 1909.

CHAPTER XIII

j. Roberts, Philip J., "Charlie Alexander," Fleming H. Revell Company, New York City, 1920.

Chapter XIV

k. Brooks, Charles A., ''Christian Americanization,'' Missionary Education Movement, New York City, 1919.

l. Attlee, C. R., ''The Social Worker,'' G. Bell, London, 1920.

m. Haggard, Rider, ''Regeneration'' (Salvation Army novel).

n. Roberts, Philip I., ''The Dry Dock of a Thousand Wrecks,'' Fleming H. Revell Company, 1912.

Chapter XV

o. Burton, Margaret E., ''Comrades in Service,'' Missionary Education Movement, New York City, 1919.

p. Fleming, Daniel Johnson, ''Marks of a World Christian,'' Associated Press, New York City, 1919.

q. Foster, Eugene C., ''Making Life Count,'' Missionary Education Movement, New York City, 1918.

r. Foster, John, ''Decision of Character,'' Student Volunteer Movement, New York City.

s. Weaver, E. W., ''Choosing an Occupation,'' Association Press, New York City, 1920.

t. Hollingworth, H. L., ''Vocational Psychology,'' D. Appleton & Co., New York City, 1916.

'ASSIGNMENTS

PART III

CHAPTER X

* What Association secretaries have you known? What most impressed you about them and their work?
* What do you consider the most important feature of Association work?

1. Why is it unusually essential in Y. W. C. A. work to "train workers about a work rather than followers about a leader"?

2. Which type of training do you consider superior for a Y. M. C. A. secretary, Association, college, or apprenticeship?

CHAPTER XI

* How many different types of field-workers have yeu met? Tell about them.

3. Point out all the distinctions you can between the work, the advantages and disadvantages, qualifications, and preparation of Christian Endeavor field-secretaries and Sunday-school field-workers.

4. As a field-worker how would you attempt to solve the "over-lapping, duplication problem"?

CHAPTER XII

5. Would you recommend the establishment of deaconess orders in all Protestant churches? Why?

6. In doing work of a similar type would you prefer to be a deaconess or a lay worker?

CHAPTER XIII

7. Name as many types of home-mission workers as you can, describing their work. (See a.)

CHAPTER XIV

8. Would you consider a salaried Red Cross worker a religious worker? Why?

9. What especially distinguishes a social-religious worker from other religious workers?

10. What can you say as to the permanence of rescue-mission conversions? (See n.)

11. What will be the result of effective prohibition upon the policy and work of the rescue mission?

CHAPTER XV

12. Prepare a different classification of religious vocations, omitting none given here and adding as many others as possible. (See a of Part I.)

13. Figure the proportionate number of women engaged in religious vocations, and make a prediction as to future increase or decrease in their number in proportion to men workers.

14. Prepare a chart showing total vocational distribution according to the estimates furnished in this book. Compare with distribution of Recruits (Appendix 4). Compare with distribution of calls.

IN GENERAL

* Which vocation do you consider most permanent? Which most transient?

15. Study and advise on case 4, case 7, case 10.

16. Select the chief difficulty and chief quality which appear most nearly distinctive of each type of worker considered.

17. Interview a worker in one of the vocations considered, and report.

18. For a special project on this section see Appendix 3.

CONCLUSION

CHAPTER XV
THE COUNSELLOR

When a young man comes to another and sincerely asks advice about his life-work, the spot where those two men stand is holy ground. Next to getting right with God is getting right with the world, and that means getting a right job. One's happiness and usefulness to himself, his family, and to society depends largely upon that. Not only getting started in the right direction, but getting started on time, is of increasing importance in this epoch, which is so decidedly a young man's age. The one who is called upon to act as counsellor is not only honored, but confronted with a great responsibility.

I. Method

In giving vocational advice go slowly. Make suggestions, but do not make decisions for other people. Encourage, but do not force issues. A man's choice of a vocation is sacred. Let him make it for himself. Above all, do not attempt to commit him to a religious vocation solely upon the grounds of the need for workers. The church ought to have volunteers who enlist because of the appeal of congenial labor and of the irresistible lure of unequalled opportunity for self-expression and service. The direct services of the counsellor are largely limited to giving information and to encouraging the inquirer in broad investigation, sincere prayer, and volunteer service as try-out measures.

The Weaver Plan. Mr. E. W. Weaver, director of occupational guidance of the united Y. M. C. A. schools, has found it helpful in talking with young people to have them prepare lists of reasons for entering a given vocation; and then he has taken the negative side in a friendly debate, himself bringing out the disadvantages. Mr. Weaver recommends the making of a plan for one's vocational future, the plan, which is to be carefully written out, to include such items as[1] the following:

1. One's preferences.
2. Reasons for one's choice.
3. Estimate of one's own qualifications.
4. List of one's recognized deficiencies and how each may be overcome.
5. Educational, financial, and physical requirements.
6. Desirable developmental employment while making preparation.
7. Schools to be attended and courses to be pursued.

Determinants of Vocational Choice. Mott finds[1] that all but nine of 828 successful ministers come from homes pronouncedly favorable to a decision for the ministry; and he reports that of 400 ministers, four-fifths give Christian parents and Christian homes as the chief factor in determining their choice. Rev. Burton St. John finds[2] in a study of 500 Student Volunteers that thirty-three per cent are influenced by conventions; twenty per cent mention home and parents; fifty-five per cent mention being helped to a decision by some person with missionary experience, while fifty-seven per cent mention the influence of other volunteers, either person-

[1]"Choosing an Occupation," Association Press, New York City, 1920, p. 12.
[2]Mott, J. R., "Future Leadership of the Church," Association Press, New York, 1909, p. 127.

ally or in small groups. As to age of decision, a study of 894 candidates for the ministry[1] indicates that 477, or fifty-three per cent, decide between the ages of sixteen and twenty-one. More studies are needed in this field.[2] Generalizations are not to be lightly made. With many exceptions, the normally advantageous age is some time between seventeen and twenty-four, perhaps; and the recruit with a Christian home as a background and the influence of a personal contact with an experienced friend as one of the main contributing influences is apt to be the one best established in his conviction, this again with many exceptions.[3]

Volunteer Work. One of the best methods of determining one's liking and fitness for a calling is through sampling the actual work. In the field of secular vocational guidance one of the keenest problems is to provide "try-out courses" which shall really approximate the actual activities of the vocational world. Industry cannot slow down while amateurs come in to experiment. In this regard the religious vocational counsellor is unusually fortunate. Volunteer church-work is everywhere always available. It affords an opportunity which should be made the most of. For many successful religious workers, volunteer church-work has proved the successful apprenticeship. McBurney, the great Y. M. C. A. secretary, decided upon a religious career as the result of winning a soul for Christ. Spurgeon preached his first sermon at sixteen as a layman. This is one secret of the great usefulness of the young people's movement in influencing life-decisions.

---

[1] Unpublished report of a study of Student Volunteers for 1919-20.
[2] Speakers' Manual, Interchurch World Movement, New York, 1920, p. 54.
[3] For a study of Christian Endeavor Recruits by the writer, see Appendix IV.

II. The Problem of Preparation

Educational preparation for religious work may be obtained in denominational colleges, in interdenominational colleges of the Bible, in Bible institutes, and in theological seminaries. The aid made available by denominational sources, ordinarily offered only to those who attend the denominational colleges and seminaries, takes the form of free tuition, annual scholarships, and loan funds. Sometimes churches provide scholarships, retaining the privilege of naming the beneficiaries. In some denominations all such help for those seeking aid comes from individual schools. Requirements and terms vary greatly.

Help from Boards. In other denominations, notably the Methodist and Presbyterian, in addition to the funds made available by separate institutions and organizations the national board of education provides assistance. Help is given to ministerial, missionary, and lay workers, the amount varying with each type of work and with each period in the schooling of each individual. In the Methodist Church a total of $600 may be borrowed during his course of preparation by any one student, interest being at four per cent. In the Presbyterian Church the usual limit is $500, with a maximum of $900 in exceptional cases. In all cases notes become due and payable within a stated period after graduation.

Recipients of aid from such loan funds are expected to show suitable character, scholarship above the average, and "prospect of promise." Notes must be given, and the applicant must have recommendation from suitable authorities. The situation is such at this time that above high-school grade any capable Recruit may reasonably hope for generous assistance in preparing for a religious carer.

III. CAUTIONS

Exceptions. "Do not despise common sense, but in the Spirit-guided life there is an uncommon sense," a statement of Rev. George Wilson's which cannot be too strongly recommended to the counsellor of Christian youth. This is but a reiteration of the point made in the introduction as to the limits in this field of religious vocations. Wesley was a failure who succeeded. Russell H. Conwell is a renowned minister who, after a successful secular career, preached his first sermon at thirty-five. When Frank Higgins,[1] martyr trail-blazer, whose life-story is destined to inspire thousands, having decided to become a preacher, set out from home, his pastor said to him, "Frank, you are making a mistake; you will make a good layman; you are not cut out for the ministry."

Especially in the matter of desirable qualities, which have been endlessly emphasized in these pages, it must be remembered that most of them are a matter of development and the working of the grace of God. The question is not only, Are these such men? but, as Robert E. Speer[2] states it: "Are they willing to let God make them such men?"

Are All Vocations Equally Christian? No honest man should ever be insulted because of his occupation. Any legitimate work that any man can ever do may be

---

[1] Whittles, Thomas D., "Frank Higgins, Trail-Blazer," Interchurch World Movement, New York, 1920, p. 23.

[2] "Wanted," in The Student Volunteer Movement Bulletin, January, 1921, p. 16.

Christian. All right work is honorable. Yet, on the other hand, one must not concede too much to the modern sentiment about the sacredness of all vocations. Through the argument that a man can serve God as well in business as in the pulpit many of the choicest and best-fitted men are missing their highest and most direct opportunity for despatching the King's business. It is possible to overemphasize Christian motive and underemphasize Christian service.

Consider two travellers. Both board the same train. Both are bound for the same city. Both are eager to arrive on time. Both are anxious for the safety of the train. Both are engaged in business. Both, in differing degrees, are indispensable to the running of the train. In almost everything these men are alike except in this: One rides in the train; the other drives it; one is a passenger; the other, the engineer. The train represents the church. To-day each qualified person has the choice of being an engineer, with his hand on the throttle, or of being simply a passenger, contributing only indirectly to the oncoming of the kingdom of God. All vocations are equally Christian, but not Christian equally to all persons. For any individual that job is most Christian for which he is best fitted and which offers him the greatest opportunity to honor and worship God and to carry out the programme of Jesus Christ for the service of society.

IV. Conclusion

"The world has had a head-on collision, and wreckage is in every corner of the earth." Humanity is knocking at the door of the church, not only for food, but for sympathy and life. This is the background. The programme is the universal brotherhood of man. The routine is ceaseless, self-spending service, helping, hoping, lifting. The indispensable quality is love, love, love. The preparation is many-sided and exacting, but it is above all such that men may take knowledge that the man trained has been with Jesus. The compensation is no Washington monument. Monuments never speak one's name aloud with tenderness, nor turn a hand to serve humanity. To leave one friend who loves and cares is better than a marble shaft; and to have wrought one's best self through Christian service into many lives to carry on when one is gone is more beautiful and difficult and permanent than the Arc de Triomphe, and this is the reward of the minister, the foreign missionary, the deaconess, and the lay worker, for the religious vocation is a sublime adventure in world friendship. Let this "advertisement" of Deaconess Hart sum up the whole story:

Wanted: Ten young women between the ages of twenty-five and thirty-five for work in the missionary district of Hankow. Applicants should possess a good digestion, a sense of humor, and an amiable disposition. Hours long, work hard, salary small, compensation wonderful.

APPENDIXES

APPENDIXES

APPENDIX I

ADDRESSES OF FOREIGN-MISSION BOARDS

BAPTIST, NORTHERN

American Baptist Foreign Mission Society, 276 Fifth Avenue, New York, N. Y.

Woman's American Baptist Foreign-Mission Society, 702 Ford Building, Boston, Mass.

BAPTIST NATIONAL CONVENTION

Lott Carey Baptist Home and Foreign Mission Convention in the United States, Phoebus, Va.

Foreign-Mission Board of the National Baptist Convention, 701 South Nineteenth Street, Philadelphia, Penn.

CONGREGATIONAL

American Board of Commissioners for Foreign Missions, 14 Beacon Street, Boston, Mass.

DISCIPLES

Personnel Secretary, College of Missions, Indianapolis, Ind.

EPISCOPAL

Domestic and Foreign Missionary Society of the Protestant Episcopal Church in the U. S. A., 281 Fourth Avenue, New York, N. Y.

METHODIST EPISCOPAL

Board of Foreign Missions of the Methodist Episcopal Church, Department of Foreign Personnel, 150 Fifth Avenue, New York, N. Y.

Woman's Foreign Missionary Society, Room 710, 150 Fifth Avenue, New York, N. Y.

METHODIST EPISCOPAL, SOUTH

Board of Missions of the Methodist Episcopal Church, South, Box 510, 810 Broadway, Nashville, Tenn.

Woman's Missionary Council of the Methodist Episcopal Church, South, 810 Broadway, Nashville, Tenn.

PRESBYTERIAN, NORTH

Board of Foreign Missions, 156 Fifth Avenue, New York, N. Y.

PRESBYTERIAN, SOUTH

Executive Committee of Foreign Missions, Box 330, 156 Fifth Avenue, North, Nashville, Tenn.

REFORMED IN THE UNITED STATES

Board of Foreign Missions, Fifteenth and Race Streets, Philadelphia, Penn.

UNITED BRETHREN

Foreign-Missionary Society, 404 Otterbein Press Building, Dayton, O.

STUDENT VOLUNTEER MOVEMENT FOR FOREIGN MISSIONS

25 Madison Avenue, New York, N. Y.

HOME-MISSION BOARDS

BAPTIST, NORTHERN

American Baptist Home-Mission Society, 23 East Twenty-sixth Street, New York, N. Y.

Woman's American Baptist Home-Mission Society, 276 Fifth Avenue, New York, N. Y.

BAPTIST, SOUTHERN

Home-Mission Board of the Southern Baptist Convention, 1004 Healey Building, Atlanta, Ga.

CONGREGATIONAL

American Missionary Association, 287 Fourth Avenue, New York, N. Y.

Congregational Home-Missionary Society, 287 Fourth Avenue, New York, N. Y.

DISCIPLES

United Christian Missionary Society, Missouri State Life Building, St. Louis, Mo.

EPISCOPAL

Domestic and Foreign Missionary Society of the Protestant Episcopal Church in the U. S. A., 281 Fourth Avenue, New York, N. Y.

METHODIST EPISCOPAL

Board of Home Missions and Church Extension, 1701 Arch Street, Philadelphia, Penn.

Woman's Home-Missionary Society, Allendale, N. J.

METHODIST EPISCOPAL, SOUTH

Home Department, General Board of Missions, Box 510, Nashville, Tenn.

Woman's Missionary Council, 810 Broadway, Nashville, Tenn.

PRESBYTERIAN, NORTH

Board of Home Missions, 156 Fifth Avenue, New York, N. Y.

Woman's Board of Home Missions, 156 Fifth Avenue, New York, N. Y.

Presbyterian Board of Publication and Sabbath-School Work, Witherspoon Building, Philadelphia, Penn.

PRESBYTERIAN, SOUTH

Executive Committee of Home Missions, 1522 Hurt Building, Atlanta, Ga.

REFORMED CHURCH IN AMERICA

Board of Domestic Missions, 25 East Twenty-second Street, New York, N. Y.

Woman's Board of Domestic Missions, 25 East Twenty-second Street, New York, N. Y.

UNITED BRETHREN

Home-Missionary Society, 412-414 Otterbein Press Building, Dayton, O.

APPENDIX II

STATISTICS

The estimates and figures presented in this book are made up from the last available statistics. Estimates are subject to great variation, and may in many cases be inaccurate; the figures upon which they are based vary from year to year, but since in the main the proportions remain fairly stable they are given here for the purpose of showing the relative distribution of religious workers. They should be sufficient for this purpose.

In the study of the foreign missionary the writer is indebted for much help to the office of William B. Tower, records, surveys, and research of the Board of Foreign Missions of the Methodist Episcopal Church. Some indication of the vocational distribution of foreign missionaries is given by a study of 1,000 ex-missionaries, furnished by Mr. Tower, which shows the following classification: Evangelists, 45 per cent; educational workers, 29 per cent; evangelistic and educational, 15 per cent; physicians, 8 per cent; nurses, 3 per cent; others, 3 per cent. The results of other investigations made by Mr. Tower for this book as to length of service and ''turn-over,'' have been indicated.

APPENDIX III

SUGGESTIONS TO STUDY-CLASS LEADERS

This book may be used for any number of sessions, preferably, perhaps, five; a preliminary session to consider the introduction, when assignments are made for Part I, which will be discussed at the second session. The fifth session may well take up the conclusion and the final discussion of the whole matter.

All starred questions are intended not for assignment, but for impromptu discussion at appropriate times. It is not expected that any one teacher will make use of all the questions. No two classes and no two teachers are alike. Some leaders may wish to prepare their own questions and assignments. Others should select those which appeal to them as significant.

In addition to the suggestions furnished at the end of each section the following features may be helpful: 1. From the very first ask all members of the class to watch for current events and clippings which bear on the subject. Prepare an exhibit of these. 2. At each session allow a short period always for general questions. If the class is large, provide a question-box. 3. In connection with the final session ask each member to prepare a report for himself on the basis of the Weaver plan. 4. In connection with the assignment which is repeated for each section of the book ''to select the chief problem and the chief desirable quality which seem distinctive of each vocation studied.'' If the class is large, have one member report for each vocation, have the reports turned in, written in briefest phrase; and then, writing each item before the class without indicating the vocation to which it is supposed to refer, have the entire class attempt to identify each one.

In addition, three special projects are suggested. For Part I, assign each vocation to a speaker, who is to make a three-minute recruiting speech. While the "three-minute squad" is speaking, the remainder of the class will sit with note-book in hand, each at the conclusion deciding to enter one of the vocations presented. The vote for each can be taken, and then different ones can be asked to state their reasons for their choice. This plan will have to be varied with the size of the class.

For Part II, select a member of the class to impersonate a candidate secretary for one of the boards of foreign missions. Select from three to six or eight persons to apply for positions for different phases of work. At least one or two of those assigned parts are to plan secretly to make such a showing at the interview as to ensure their rejection. During the several interviews, which may consume about thirty to thirty-five minutes, the class sit with pencil and paper, prepared at the close to pass judgment upon the applications, accepting or rejecting them.

For Part III, each member of the class may be asked to prepare a fifty-word "help-wanted" advertisement for at least one vocation presented in that section. Or some few may be given this assignment, the remainder by secret ballot deciding which advertisement is best.

These special projects will be especially useful in large classes because they will utilize large numbers in the briefest possible time, bringing out essential points of the text. Leaders should use their own ingenuity in devising other and better projects. Projects are especially valuable in teaching because they stimulate interest, they encourage each member of the class to appropriate, to attack, to work over, to use the book effectively, and to contribute something of himself to the class discussions rather than an assignment from the text. Not to memorize the book, but to use it with interest, is the essential thing. To awaken a new point of view and to stimulate keen interest, self-activity on the part of the members is indispensable.

APPENDIX IV

CASES OF LIFE-WORK RECRUITS

Of 307 Life-Work Recruits recently enrolled by the United Society of Christian Endeavor, 40 per cent are men. The fields of service chosen by this group of 307 are as follows: Foreign missions, 126; the ministry, 50; undecided, 33; young people's work, 17; social settlement, 16; evangelism, 16; home missions, 14; church secretary, 7; nursing, 7; singing evangelist, 5; teaching, 4; Y. W. C. A., 4; religious education, 4; Y. M. C. A., 3; deaconess, 1.

The writer selected 150 Recruits from Maine to Texas, at the ratio of four men to six women. Replies were received from only 31 women and 25 men. The ages of the 31 women ranged from thirteen to forty-two, with the average at twenty-two, 44 per cent falling in the four years between sixteen and twenty-one. In reply to the question as to what had most influenced their life-work decision nine placed a convention address first, six placed it second, and five placed the home first. Of the women, eighteen mention a convention address, seven mention home. The ages of the men varied from fifteen to thirty-one, with the average at twenty-one and one-half, 56 per cent falling between sixteen and twenty-one. In answer to the above question, six placed the pastor first and six placed the home first. Of the men, thirteen mention home, eleven mention the pastor. A comparison of the men and the women is interesting, although the number of questionnaires is far too small to warrant any generalizations.

The following cases are selected and compiled from the personal, anonymous statements of forty-two Christian Endeavor Life-Work Recruits who replied to the request to state their cases.

CASE 1 (WOMAN)

"I am twenty-one. I worked my way through high school. Through a missionary, home on furlough, I learned of the difficulties and need for doctors and nurses. I decided to enlist for foreign service. My family are very much opposed to my selection. I get no encouragement from them, but I hope for a change in attitude in answer to my prayers.

"I would have started to college this fall; but my health was not extra good, and I felt I could not earn my way and study hard. I am going to Chicago to take a nurses' training-course. I have a brother in college whom I am helping. I have five younger brothers and sisters whom I am also trying to help through school."

CASE 2 (MAN)

"I am twenty, and have chosen the ministry because I have a personal liking for it. I graduated from high school, and have spent one year in college. This year I am staying out on account of poor health. The doctor advised outdoor life, and I have a job reading water-meters. I hope to continue college next September.

"Personal fitness worries me a great deal. I know that I am only a one-talent man. Furthermore, I am not sure but that my desire to enter the ministry is purely selfish. It attracts me greatly. I have always wanted to be a preacher, and thought that I would enjoy it more than anything else. Perhaps I have not a call. I have talked a great deal about this with my grandmother, who believes that I should wait until I receive a call in some unmistakable manner, and can no longer doubt of my fitness."

CASE 3 (WOMAN)

"I am just twenty. I am undecided, but I want to be a medical missionary. I made my decision on the spur of the moment without having talked it over with my parents. I was happy at first; but later I realized the spirit of the convention had carried me away, and I had done wrong not to consult with any one.

"When I got home, I told mother I had given my life to Jesus. She said, 'You have done that already.' When I explained I meant life-work, and wanted to be a missionary, she said she couldn't let me go. This is all the talk I have ever had with my parents.

"I'm in my second year of college, and my folks expect me to teach. However, I have always wanted to be a doctor, and feel that I could best serve the Lord that way. Last year I took up pre-medical work, but dropped it this year. My parents opposed me, and I know they would not let me go to foreign lands. I am very fond of children, and I would like to find some work with them if I cannot go as a medical missionary."

CASE 4 (MAN)

"I am twenty; and am undecided what to do, although I have entered a denominational college. Would like to be a minister, but question my success. My mother is a widow, and I am the only child. As long as she lives I would not like to go to a foreign field. I believe I would be more successful as a teacher than as a preacher.

"I have been an Endeavor worker for four years. I have travelled up and down the State doing different kinds of Christian Endeavor work. For two years I have been State Intermediate superintendent. I have also made several trips with State officers, acting as song-leader and general utility man. The State field-secretary will tell you about me."

CASE 5 (MAN)

"I am twenty-one; talents and qualifications fit me best, I believe, for the ministry. At the age of eighteen I enlisted in the United States army, and served nine months in France. I had no relatives left, and was anxious to go. After two terrible months on the front line I was sent to that 'hell hole' at Brest to embark for home; but I ended up in the hospital with 'flu' and pleurisy.

"While I was in the army I had many opportunities to witness successfully for Jesus. I many times prayed with men, and never failed to read my Bible daily, sometimes to others. I like the discipline of army life, and my sympathy and friendship go out to the men in uniform. If I did not feel a call to the ministry, I believe I would re-enlist in the army now, for I have great faith in the manhood of the service.''

CASE 6 (MAN)

''I am eighteen, and I have decided to be a missionary because of the influence of a saintly teacher who herself once planned to go as a missionary, but was kept home through duty to a weak sister and a dependent father. Her cherished ideal she gave up, substituting in its place an ambition to send some one in her place. I am that one, who since her sudden death am more determined than ever 'to carry on.'

''My folks object to my taking up the work, my grandfather offering to pay my college expenses if I will become a lawyer. If I do not accept, I must earn my own way through school. My line of work seems to lie in organizing, as I have made several defunct organizations going concerns. I would like very much the work of a Y. M. C. A. secretary or Christian Endeavor secretary here at home, and maybe I could accomplish more here than in foreign service. I do not know what to do.''

CASE 7 (WOMAN)

''I am twenty-one; Christian Endeavor and its fellowship with consecrated workers is responsible for my decision. Several things have been problems, but in His time most of them have been worked out. Before signing, two drawbacks were present—home and fiancé. But prayer overcame them, and my friend is now a Recruit, studying for the ministry. My home influence has been changed so my parents are glad if I can serve. I'm not decided as to work. My problem is finding my place and knowing just what preparation it requires.''

CASE 8 (MAN)

''I am now twenty-one, and I have become a Life-Work Recruit through the influence of my pastor's sermons, through a chum, and because of a convention address which I heard last year. I would like to enter the ministry or foreign-missionary service; but financial considerations, securing preparation, and doubts of personal fitness stand in the way.

"It is so difficult to learn. I have always been at the foot of the class. I just cannot accomplish what I should and want to. Everything comes slow. I studied from half-past five mornings until half-past eleven evenings. Frequently I stayed at school until six o'clock. I did, however, graduate when I was seventeen from the grade school.

"I am now taking a normal industrial-training course. I am earning my own way. It has been necessary for me to clean cellars, wash windows, haul coal, carry out furniture. I am now working in an apartment-house, hours seven at night to half-past seven in the morning, caring for switchboard, boiler, distributing papers, and running errands."

CASE 9 (WOMAN)

"I am thirty-two, and I wish to go as a foreign missionary. I grew tired of the butterfly life about me, and decided to make my life count for something. I had so often fallen far short of the self that I wanted to be that at the last State convention the decision service came to me as a challenge to give myself up entirely. I am teaching; my mother is entirely dependent upon me for support.

"Am I too old to go now to the foreign field, even if I could prepare and could have my mother provided for? I do not know what to do. I should think there would be some sort of organization which would advise Recruits for what type of work they might prepare."

CASE 10 (MAN)

"I am nineteen, and a sophomore at the State university. I am undecided, but think I'll study law. I became a Recruit three years ago through the influence of my home, principally. My father is a minister. In my senior year at high school I was elected class president. But I had just become a Recruit, and, when I thought over all my duties, I discovered that I would have to take the leading rôle in planning dances and other questionable amusements. I immediately got down on my knees, and asked

God to guide me. The next day my prayer was answered. I called a special meeting of the class, and resigned. The class tried to argue with me that I could delegate to a committee the dances. Their argument was to no avail. After my stand the secretary and one other officer also withdrew through my stand for the right.

"I made the varsity football team last fall. I want to put my life where it will count most, but I do not believe the ministry is the place. I believe I can have a wider influence for Christ in the profession of the law, out in the world among men."

www.ingramcontent.com/pod-product-compliance
Lightning Source LLC
Chambersburg PA
CBHW032116040426
42449CB00005B/165